CALL TO THE CENTER

By the same author

CALLED: *New Thinking on Christian Vocation*

DAILY WE TOUCH HIM: *Practical Religious Experiences*

CENTERING PRAYER: *Renewing an Ancient Christian Prayer Form*

CENTERED LIVING: *The Way of Centering Prayer*

THOMAS MERTON, BROTHER MONK: *The Quest of True Freedom*

THE EUCHARIST YESTERDAY AND TODAY

IN PETER'S FOOTSTEPS: *Learning to Be a Disciple* (The paperback edition of this book is entitled DAILY WE FOLLOW HIM: *Learning Discipleship from Peter.)*

JUBILEE: *A Monk's Journal*

O HOLY MOUNTAIN: *Journal of a Retreat on Mount Athos*

CHALLENGES IN PRAYER

MONASTERY

LAST OF THE FATHERS

BREAKING BREAD: *The Table Talk of Jesus*

A MANUAL OF LIFE: *The New Testament for Daily Reading*

MARY TODAY: *Challenging Woman, Model for Maturing Christians*

PRAYERTIMES—MORNING—MIDDAY—EVENING: *A Pocket "Liturgy of the Hours" for All Christians*

THROUGH THE YEAR WITH THE SAINTS: *A Daily Companion for Private or Liturgical Prayer,*

A RETREAT WITH THOMAS MERTON

LIVING OUR PRIESTHOOD TODAY

LONG ON THE JOURNEY: *Reflections of a Pilgrim*

CALL
TO THE
CENTER

*The Gospel's Invitation
to Deeper Prayer*

M. Basil Pennington, O.C.S.O.

AN IMAGE BOOK
DOUBLEDAY
NEW YORK   LONDON   TORONTO   SYDNEY   AUCKLAND

AN IMAGE BOOK
PUBLISHED BY DOUBLEDAY
a division of Bantam Doubleday Dell Publishing Group, Inc.
666 Fifth Avenue, New York, New York 10103

IMAGE, DOUBLEDAY, and the portrayal of a cross
intersecting a circle are trademarks of Doubleday, a
division of Bantam Doubleday Dell Publishing Group, Inc.

Library of Congress Cataloging-in-Publication Data
Pennington, M. Basil.
Call to the center : the Gospel's invitation to
    deeper prayer / M. Basil Pennington. — 1st ed.
        p.   cm.
    "Image books."
    1. Bible. N.T. Matthew—Meditations.
2. Devotional calendars—Catholic Church.
3. Catholic Church—Doctrines.   4. Contemplation–
Biblical teaching.   I. Title.
BS2575.5.P46   1990   89-35031
242'.5—dc20   CIP
ISBN 0-385-24679-X

*To David
with special love*

Contents

8 CONTENTS

Preface

A Word to Friends

It has been my tremendous and undeserved privilege to share something of the grace I have received in the contemplative life with many in the form of "centering prayer." It is said that the best way to learn something is to teach it. Certainly I have learned many things about prayer, about what it means to be human and Christian and about the human journey as I have shared something of my journey in prayer and the simple method that opens the way for that journey. Of course, I have never really taught prayer. Only the Spirit of the Lord can teach us how to pray: *"We do not know how to pray as we ought, but the Holy Spirit prays within us."* I have just had the joy of sharing a very simple, ancient method found in our Christian tradition which enables us to open the space for the Spirit to begin to pray in us the way she wishes.

In the course of our centering prayer workshops, I have always kept the Sacred Scriptures enthroned in our midst as a real presence and have regularly turned to them for "a Word from our Sponsor." In the course of most workshops we have also had the joy of celebrating the Eucharist together. And this has given us another opportunity to listen to the Scriptures in the context of our centering.

The Word of God is living. It is not just a text, however inspired. It is the Word himself, present now in our midst and speaking to us here and now. And he speaks to us where we are at the moment. Thus, in the moments when we turned to the Word during the centering prayer workshops, he inevitably spoke to us about centering. Over the course of the past fifteen years I have had many, many opportunities, then, to hear the Word speak about centering—about this call to the center.

On many occasions participants have asked me if I had published the Word I was sharing. The answer was necessarily no, for it was a living Word that the Lord, then and there, was speaking. A few of them have shown up in the books I have published on centering prayer. Many more have been captured on tape. (One of the delightful phenomena of our times is that at the end of a talk you are not greeted with applause until first you are greeted with the click of many tape recorders completing their important task. You can time your talk by the tapes: the C30s get flipped at fifteen minutes; at thirty minutes, they get replaced and the C60s get flipped; at forty-five minutes, the C30s are getting flipped again along with the C90s. If you go an hour, the C30s and the C60s are both being pulled out and it is surely time to quit.)

Responding to the request of many, I have here gathered up some of the fragments from the workshops. And I have added a few others that have come to me in my more private moments with the Lord.

There is inevitably a certain amount of repetition as we move through the commentaries. Although I did do *some* editing, I've allowed some repetition to remain. A given Scriptural passage, seen in different contexts, can open up wholly new insights.

Our tradition has spoken of three kinds of contemplation. There is the *direct:* one plunges directly into the Divine. Centering prayer itself is this sort of contemplation. There is the *oblique:* we reach to the Divine through his creation, through his effects. We walk along a wintry road and the sun begins to emerge over the horizon, peeking through the nude trees, shyly warming, not hurting the eyes, drawing our whole attention; so it is with the God who loves us. And finally, there is the *circular:* we circle around the Reality, catching a glimpse here and a glimpse there, each adding to the overall impression, until finally we are drawn in and possessed by the Reality itself. This little book is an exercise in the circular.

Centering prayer is listening to a call—*the* call—letting everything else go, simply listening: *"Be still and know that I am God."*

These encounters with the Word of God in his inspired Scriptures are a listening. We are circling around the One who calls. We hear his words, we feel the tug of his enticements, we enter into his images. Little by little, it does get home to us that our God, the God, the Almighty, the Infinite All, does indeed want to enter into most intimate communion with us. He is a loving Lord, a loving Father, a Lover—our Lover. This is *the* message of the God who walked arm in arm with Adam in the Garden of Eden, who set his arc in the heavens for Noah, who called Abraham out of Ur, who wrestled with Jacob, who delivered Joseph. This is what Moses heard in the Burning Bush, and what judges, prophets, and kings heard again and again. This is the message of the Incarnation: God became human so that humans could become God and be his friends. This is the why of Church, of sacraments, of priesthood, and of Eucharist. This is why he draws men and women apart to "waste" their lives in the cloister. And this is something of the why of many of the deprivations of human life—a hard saying—of handicaps, bereavements, sickness, isolation. Not that God causes these things. He gives us our freedom, and we use it in the stupid and sinful ways that we do. Yet he knows that he will yet turn all things to good. These crosses offer the possibility of passing beyond to the tomb, the death of the false self, so that we can rise to a new life, a life where we hear our "Mary," our name, and know our Master and know that there is for us an eternal, undying love that reaches even beyond the tomb.

So journey with me for a while. I would suggest that this is not a book to be read through. Rather, it is for daily *lectio.* It is a book for listening. First, call upon the Spirit—the Holy Spirit dwelling in you, who lives in these living Words. Ask her to make them live for you. Then listen to the chosen pericope. Take your time. If a particular word, phrase, or sentence speaks to you, don't hurry on. Stay with it. Let it resonate in your depths. Don't try to figure it out. Or store it away for future reference (for that homily you have to preach, for that article you are going to write, or for somebody else who needs it). Don't try to wring out of it all the emotional juice you can. Just let it be there. Let the mind descend into the heart and form it, calling forth its response. Rest in that response, in the Reality. Then when you are ready, move on. If that is all you have time for today—OK. There is tomorrow. You can begin the pericope again. You have met the Lord. He has spoken his Word to you. What more do you want?

After you have listened to the pericope to the end, be for a time with yourself and with the Lord. Don't rush on to my words. The Lord may have his own particular Word for you. Only when you have taken the time for that, move on to our faith-sharing.

Again, take your time. Gather up the fragments one by one, and savor them. True, at some point you may want to get the overall impression. Fine.

This is meant to be the kind of book that you can return to again and again. A companion book that will nourish and support your daily centering. A book for group sharing, opening the space for your centering prayer group to share their own experience of the Word. However, what is offered here is but so many sips from an inexhaustible Source. I offer only thirty pericopes from the Gospel of Saint Matthew—one for each day of the month, if you will —following along in the text to the summit of Tabor, a fitting place to rest. I hope you will go on to the rest of Matthew and then the other Evangelists, letting the Spirit herself teach you as only she can.

Greater things than I have seen, you will see; greater things than I have heard, you will hear.

Father Basil
Assumption Abbey
Easter 1989

CALL TO THE CENTER

Chapter 1

❖

The Wise Still Seek Him

After Jesus had been born at Bethlehem in Judea during the reign of King Herod, suddenly some wise men came to Jerusalem from the east, asking, "Where is the infant king of the Jews? We saw his star as it rose and have come to do him homage." When King Herod heard this he was perturbed, and so was the whole of Jerusalem. He called together all the chief priests and the scribes of the people, and enquired of them where the Christ was to be born. They told him, "At Bethlehem in Judea, for this is what the prophet wrote:

> And you, Bethlehem, in the land of Judah,
> you are by no means the *least among the leaders*
>   *of Judah,*
> for *from you will come a leader*
> who will *shepherd* my people Israel."

Then Herod summoned the wise men to see him privately. He asked them the exact date on which the star had appeared and sent them on to Bethlehem with the words, "Go and find out all about the child, and when you have found him, let me know, so that I too may go and do him homage." Having listened to what the king had to say, they set out. And suddenly the star they had seen rising went forward and halted over the place where the child was. The sight filled them with delight, and going into the house they saw the child with his mother Mary, and falling to their knees they did him homage. Then, opening their treasures, they offered him gifts of gold and frankincense and myrrh. But they were given a warning in a dream not to go back to Herod, and returned to their own country by a different way.

Matthew 2:1–12

Not too long ago we witnessed many from among us heading east, following a "star," hoping to find some "wise men" who could lead them to the Source of all wisdom. This was not a wholly new phenomenon, to say the least. History does repeat itself, again and again. Way back in the fourth century, my own patron, Saint Basil of Caesarea, and his friend Gregory were studying in the academies of Athens and not finding what they were seeking: true wisdom. So they chucked their books and headed east, into Mesopotamia, Syria, Palestine, and Egypt. They were not alone in this. John Cassian, the Dalmatian, had the same sort of frustrating experience at Rome and journeyed eastward. Centering prayer is the fruit of his long journeying to sources of wisdom, the fathers and mothers of the desert. Women went that way too. There was Paula and that delightful couple Melania the Elder and her granddaughter, Melania the Younger.

Indeed, we can go back to yet an earlier time in our tradition. What were John and Andrew doing on the eastern side of the Jordan, these fishermen from the shores of the Sea of Galilee? Young men, with seeking hearts, they had heard there was someone over there who might have some answers.

But they were sent back across the Jordan. Even in our times, the wisest of the masters have sent searchers back to their own roots and sources. The wise men of the Gospels were led to the west. Or perhaps it is truer to say, to the center. For if there is any place in this world that can be considered "the center," it is *the* Holy City—Jerusalem. Between east and west, belonging to both, it was God's chosen dwelling place on earth, the place to which he drew his Chosen People.

Yet, the Holy City of old was not the end of the quest for these wise men. Perhaps it was too lofty and exalted. Perhaps it had compromised too much with the values of this passing world to keep its heart centered. Yet the Church was still centered there. There one could find the authentic Scriptures. And there they would be authentically interpreted.

The Scriptures would point the way.

Centering prayer begins with faith: *"Be in faith and love . . ."* And "faith comes through hearing"—hearing the Word of God. The wise men were led to the right place. We, too, must turn to the Scriptures, the Scriptures that are authenticated by the living authority of the Tradition. This is the twofold source—which is one—of that revelation of God's intimate love for us that calls us to the center, to the place of intimate encounter with the living God, the

Source of all wisdom and peace and love, of all that we seek and long for.

Bethlehem, the "House of Bread," is the place.

We must remember that the Scriptures always have several levels of meaning. Besides the literal or historical meaning, Scripture has allegorical or deeper spiritual meanings. Jerusalem is a city in Palestine, situated on Mount Sion. But Jerusalem is also the heavenly city, the one that will come down from above as the bride of Christ (Rv 21:2). It is the mystical city that is forming even now on earth among the faithful; it is the Church.

There are then mystical meanings to the inspired word that are meant to teach and guide us. We want to be attentive to them.

Bethlehem is the House of Bread. The place to which the star leads us, that inner place, the place to which we are called, is the place where we will be fed, a house of bread, if we will but go there and dwell so that our spirit can be nourished. If we but let him, God will satisfy all our desires, satiate all our hunger. "Behold, I stand at the door and knock. If one will open, I will come in and sit with him, side by side, and share a meal with him." (Rv 3:20)

We are, in some senses, the least. Or so it might seem. In some ways we are worse than the least. We have been made to the very image of God. And more, we have been brought into union with the very Son of God, a union that is beyond anything we can comprehend. We, of whom all this is true, have yet sinned, have failed in so many ways to live up to the reality of who we are. We are the least. And yet, within us dwells a leader, *the* Leader of God's People, indeed, God himself, the Shepherd of Israel. God's option for the poor never ceases. Centering, we can enter within this least place and find all we are seeking.

The wise men had turned to the Scriptures and to the authentic interpreters of those Scriptures. Now they could safely proceed. Now they had direction. And then their star reappeared and seemed to give them clearer direction than before. Grace, the Revelation, and the guidance of the Church do not replace our natural gifts and talents. They act within these and give them a renewed clarity and power. At the same time, the wounds within us which inhibit the full and free activity of our human faculties, our reason and our will, will by that very fact also inhibit the free working of grace within us. This is why the deep healing we find in centering prayer is so important. We can make a decision to follow the path marked out for us in seeking Christ, but if the energies within us have been habitually ordered to seeking our own security, pleasure, and power, the effectiveness of our decision is going to be greatly impaired until we are freed from the old habitual orientation and are free to follow the new.

The wise men—wise men indeed—were free men. They had been able to leave their own land and its habitual security, accept the discomforts of the long, arduous journey, and submit to the vicissitudes of traveling in a foreign land and submitting to an authority, in order to seek him who had in some mysterious way grasped their hearts.

"Seek and you shall find."

They persevered until the end. If we persevere in our practice, once the living Tradition has shown us the way of centering prayer, we, too, shall find.

". . . they saw the child with his mother Mary . . ."

Sometimes good Catholics are a bit disturbed by what they perceive to be one aspect of centering prayer: Mary is left out. That is only a misperception. Jesus is always found with his mother. It is through Mary that God entered into our humanity. It is through Mary that he always comes to us humans. But Mary does not want attention focused upon herself. She may at times have a very central place in our spiritual journey, usually early on. Little ones need a mother. We are always little; we always need Mary. Yet, in ways, we do grow and her role in our life changes. Very readily does she fade as it were into the background so that we can center more totally on her Son. When we come to the center, though, we do not find only God. We find ourselves and all the others who come forth from his creative love. And we find no one there more fully than Mary, for no one of us, his beloved creatures, so expresses his creative love as does this all-holy woman whom he himself calls Mother. Mary is not absent from our centering. She, the mediatrix of all graces, is very present. But during our time of intimate embrace, our time of centering, she does not want us to fix our attention on her but wants us to love the Lord our God with our whole mind, whole heart, whole soul, and whole strength, as she does. And she is there to help us do just that in her own most loving and hidden way.

". . . and falling to their knees they did him homage."

I do not think we can really come to true adoration until we have come to the center, to the true self, and left behind all the limitations of the false self. As long as we approach God through our own limited concepts, symbols, or images, we are far too shielded from his awesomeness. When we have the courage to leave these security blankets behind and open the space for him himself to be present to us, then indeed all we can do is fall down in homage. No words quite say what we would want to say. Our gestures are poor. No gift is really enough. We can only give him our whole being in homage. We have nothing more. But then there is nothing more that he wants from us. Indeed, it is this for which he created us. All else he can equally well get from someone else. But no one can give him ourselves. This we alone can give him. And this is what he wants from us—all that we are. So that he can fill all that we are with his ineffable love and joy.

The wise men offered him their symbolic gifts of gold and frankincense and myrrh. Gold spoke of security. From wealth and what it can purchase we seek a security that, in the end, proves ephemeral and false. Frankincense speaks of power, the adulation that it brings, a sense of almost being a god. The power our false self seeks to grasp and hold on to is in fact quickly consumed, going up in smoke and not even leaving a fragrant scent, only the ashes of broken careers and broken lives. And myrrh possesses a pungent, sensual sweetness. Like all the sensual pleasures of this world, it has a bitterness at the heart of it. Myrrh is associated with death. In giving over our quest for pleasure and sensual satisfaction, we do indeed die to self, the false self. It can be very painful, especially if it is the only self we know. But it is the only way to the powerful, wonderful, secure, free life of the true self.

The wise men gave over all to the One they found in the nourishing Center. And they were rewarded with yet more. They returned to their everyday world "by a different way." They now saw life with very different eyes. They had seen and experienced the ultimate meaning of it all. They were free, healed, and whole.

If we faithfully go to the center with the attitude of the wise men, offering the Lord our gold (all our false securities and need for them), our frankincense (all our need for a sense of power and the adulation that comes with it), and our myrrh (all our cravings for sensual pleasures), we, too, will come to life by a different way, a way that will be marked by the fruits of the Spirit: love, joy, peace, patience, and all the other fruits of the Spirit, as we see more and more, in all and through all and with all, the Lord and ourselves one with him.

Chapter 2

❖

Space for the Spirit

Then Jesus appeared: he came from Galilee to the Jordan to be baptized by John. John tried to dissuade him, with the words, "It is I who need baptism from you, and yet you come to me!" But Jesus replied, "Leave it like this for the time being; it is fitting that we should, in this way, do all that uprightness demands." Then John gave in to him. And when Jesus had been baptized he at once came up from the water, and suddenly the heavens opened and he saw the Spirit of God descending like a dove and coming down on him. And suddenly there was a voice from heaven. "This is my Son, the Beloved; my favor rests on him." Then Jesus was led by the Spirit out into the desert to be put to the test by the devil.

Matthew 3:13–4:1

It doesn't really make too much sense, does it? At least speaking from our usual human vantage point. The Master comes to the disciple, the Lord to the servant, the All-Holy

One to one of his sinful creatures—and comes seeking to undergo a rite of purification.

"Leave it like this for the time being . . ."

We come faithfully to our daily encounter with the Lord in the depths of our being. We know he is here. Our faith, weak and poor though it may be, yet assures us of his presence. And yet he seems to be in no way present.

There are two kinds of love. There is the love of pleasure or enjoyment, when we are in the presence of the one whom we love. We are fulfilled. Our heart's desire is realized. Everything is complete. Our beloved is here. And then there is the love of desire, when our beloved is perceived as absent. Our whole being longs for the absent one. We are certainly far from being satisfied or fulfilled.

God is always present in us. Otherwise we would simply cease to exist. At every moment, he brings us forth in his creative love, sharing with us something of his own very being. But he likes to play hide-and-seek. Read again that magnificent piece of ancient love poetry, the Song of Songs. So often when we sit down to center, the Lord seems quite simply to have disappeared. He does this so that we will abide in the love of desire.

The love of presence is complete. We have what we want. There is no striving or seeking. We do not grow. We rest, and rest content. But with the love of desire, our whole being is restless; we are sometimes very aware of this during our centering. We are seeking and striving to find, to be with, to enjoy him whom our soul loves. When we sit in the love of desire, as we so often do in our centering, our love grows and is purified. We would much rather enjoy the love of presence. But the Lord says to us, as he said to John, "Leave it like this for the time being."

We may not see our need for further purification. Have we not already come a long way? What a change there has been in our lives. Most people would consider us pretty far advanced, spending time in contemplative prayer twice a day everyday. We really do want the Lord. Doesn't he know that?

Indeed, he does. That is why he trusts us and dares to leave us in this longing, which some call darkness or dryness. He knows our deep desire for him, and he is responding to us. For it is only in this experience of the love of desire that our love does grow and, with it, our capacity to receive him more and more fully into our being and into our lives. There is absolutely no limit from the side of God to how much he can give us himself and his joy and his life, this God of infinite love. All the limitations are on our side. And these limitations do not come from our nature. We have been made in the very image of God. We are made for, and long for, infinite love, the love that only God can give. Only he can satisfy the longing that we are. But we do not know ourselves and we do not know our God. We think we can find what we are looking for elsewhere than in God. We look for it in ourselves and in others. We do not know our God—that he is, indeed, our God and our all. We think we need other things besides him. And in seeking those other things, we block his full entrance into our lives.

As we sit here in the love of desire, those other things that vie to fill our lives (and actually do clutter them) rise up one after the other. In a most subtle way, the Lord keeps saying to us, "Do you love me more than this?" As we gently return to him with our love word, we make our choice. And in that choosing, we let go of the other. There is more room in us for the infinite love to invade us. Our very being expands to receive him.

There is no limit to the amount of purification that we each need. The achieving of complete purity of heart is a lifetime's work. For most, it won't even be completed here. The Catholic Church has the consoling doctrine of purgatory, a place where this purification can be completed. We happily have no need of reincarnation and going through a lifelong journey again. If we are truly faithful to opening ourselves to the divine therapy that is worked in us in contemplative prayer, complete purity of heart will be brought about in us. As soon as that is complete, we will enter into the heavenly realm of being.

So when we go to our centering and find ourselves sitting there wanting God and he apparently nowhere in sight, sitting there in darkness or dryness (choose your own image), sitting there like a bump on a log, *leave it like this for the time being; it is fitting that we should* . . . Like John, let us give in to the Lord.

When we do, we open the space for the Holy Spirit. The heavens open for us and the Spirit of God comes upon us. Actually, the Holy Spirit is always there, one with the Father and Son, dwelling in us, bringing us into being, waiting for us to come home to ourselves to enjoy their divine presence. What we do do when we sit there, letting go of all our thoughts and feelings and images, is this: we open space for the Spirit to begin to act within us.

One of our problems is that God is "a perfect gentleman"—or maybe I should say, "a perfect lady." God knows us as no one else does. He knows us through and through. And he knows that the greatest thing about us is our freedom, for herein is our power to love. And God is love. God respects our freedom more than anyone else. He will never force his way into our lives. As he says in the last book of the revelation: "Behold, I stand at the door and knock. And *if* one opens, I will come in." He will not force his way in.

Why did God make you? I imagine there immediately comes to the minds of many the old catechism answer: He made me to know, love, and serve him in this world and be happy with him in the next. That answer actually contains a bit of heresy and has probably caused more people to leave God and the Church behind than anything else written. Even as a little one, I found it hard to understand how I could love God and not be happy with him. A god who wants us to keep our noses to the grindstone in service all life long and come to enjoy him and be happy with him only in the hereafter is not an attractive god. In fact, he is a very unattractive god and certainly not our God of infinite joy and love.

God the Father, God the Son, and God the Holy Spirit were infinitely happy. They were "having a ball"—an unending one. But when we are happy the one thing we do want is to be able to share our happiness with others. God wanted someone, or rather someones, with whom he could share his infinite happiness, his godly happiness.

At the monastery I have a wonderful little dog. His name is Diers. Each morning I go out for a walk after Mass. When I come out, Diers comes running up to me, jumps up gleefully, and, in his effort to kiss me, slobbers on my beard. Then he goes skipping down the road before me. We are great friends. But when I have a special joy, some happiness I really want to share, I do not go out to the doghouse to do it. No, I seek one of my brothers, who can fully enter into my joy. Diers just doesn't have what it takes to enter into fully human joy and happiness.

However, if some fairy godmother came along and bopped little Diers on the head with her magic wand and turned him into a human, and then endowed him with our human powers of understanding, willing, and feeling, then my little friend could fully enter into my joys and be the best of friends, a true companion for the journey.

There is a far greater distance, though, between God and me than there is between Diers and me. But at baptism, God, not a fairy godmother, bopped you and me on the head as some good friend poured the divinizing waters over us. We were made partakers of the divine nature, raised up to the divine level by participation in God's own life and being. God's own Spirit was given to us to be our spirit. And, so that we could function at this new level, at the divine level, we were given a whole new set of faculties through which the Holy Spirit as our spirit could function. Traditionally these are called the gifts of the Holy Spirit— "gifts" because they are gratuitously given and "of the Spirit" because they are the faculties through which she operates in our lives.

Most of us most of the time leave these gifts wrapped up on the shelf. Insisting on operating according to our own human faculties, our reason, imagination, and feelings, we do not leave space in our lives for the Holy Spirit to operate in us through the gifts she has given us. In centering, we begin to leave aside our own thoughts and images and feelings and to make space for the Holy Spirit to begin to operate in us through the gifts. We begin to see things as

God sees them, sense them the way he does. We are able to enter into his happiness. Something of his infinite joy begins to take hold in us. And also all those other fruits of the Spirit of which Saint Paul speaks: love, peace, kindness, long-suffering, patience, benignity.

This begins to happen not only during the time of our prayer. Once the Spirit sees that we really want her to act in our lives through her gifts, she begins to act in us more and more. Outside the time of prayer, we begin—and often others begin before us—to perceive the presence of these wonderful fruits in our daily lives. These are the fruits by which we judge the "tree" of our centering prayer. We can not judge the prayer in itself, for the level at which it takes place is beyond that which the rational mind can perceive and judge. It is only through these fruits and the healing they represent that we can know the Spirit is working in our lives through this deep, quiet communion with God at the center of our being.

When we begin to function in this way, the Father then does see us as his Son, as men and women who have been baptized into Christ, brought into a oneness with him that is more intimate than anything we can conceive, a oneness like unto the oneness that the Son does have with the Father. He says of each one of us, "This is my Son, the Beloved; my favor rests on him."

". . . led by the Spirit . . ."

And like Jesus, we will be more and more led by the Spirit. Through the gifts of knowledge, understanding, wisdom, and counsel, she will be active in our lives. We will come to know things as they are seen by God and the meanings that have been revealed to us through Jesus, the Scriptures, and the living Tradition. We will come to be perceptive of what "stands under," of the divine presence and activity in all persons and things. We will come to sense God in all. The Latin word for "wisdom" is *sapientia,* coming from the root *sapor,* to savor or taste. As the Lord says in the Psalms, "Taste and see how sweet is the Lord." With new perception we will come to make the decisions in our lives with something of the wisdom that comes from God himself.

We will be led by the Spirit, but that does not mean the end of the problems, trials, and temptations of life. We will be put to the test, but with the help of the Spirit, even as we are tested, we will see more clearly what are temptations that can lead us away from God. And we will see how we can respond to these with the ever-powerful Word of God.

Chapter 3

❖

Not by Bread Alone

Then Jesus was led by the Spirit out into the desert to be put to the test by the devil. He fasted for forty days and forty nights, after which he was hungry, and the tester came and said to him, "If you are the Son of God, tell these stones to turn into loaves." But he replied, "Scripture says:

> Human beings live not on bread alone
> but on every word that comes from the mouth
>   of God."

The devil then took him to the holy city and set him on the parapet of the Temple. "If you are the Son of God," he said, "throw yourself down; for Scripture says:

> He has given his angels orders about you,
> and they will carry you in their arms
> in case you trip over a stone."

Jesus said to him, "Scripture also says:

> Do not put the Lord your God to the test."

Next, taking him to a very high mountain, the devil

showed him all the kingdoms of the world and their splendour. And he said to him, "I will give you all these, if you fall at my feet and do me homage." Then Jesus replied, "Away with you, Satan! For Scripture says:

> The Lord your God is the one to whom you must
>   do homage,
> him alone you must serve."

The devil left him, and suddenly angels appeared and looked after him.

Matthew 4:1–11

We have to go into the desert, leaving the world and all its doings behind. That is where the Spirit leads each one of us, one way or another. If we are going to respond to the leadings of God—which is the only way to true happiness —then we must go.

It is literally the desert to which some are led. Abba Matta is welcoming hundreds to Scete in Egypt and fathers them there now. The spiritual sons and daughters of Charles de Foucauld, "the Hermit of the Sahara," have their times in the desert. The Cistercian nuns at Senoita in Arizona look out on vast stretches of desert sand and know something of the solitude of God.

In a very real way, all monks and nuns are called to the desert. The true monastic life, with its many traditional renouncements, gives its followers even in urban monasteries a certain emptiness and space—a space for the Divine.

A prolonged illness is sometimes a desert that suddenly encircles some. A sickroom or even a bed can be a vast solitude, especially when the illness is one that carries a certain stigma with it, as many victims of AIDS have come to experience.

The loneliness of large-city dwelling, the soaring heights and endless corridors of barricaded apartment doors, the fears of the night and of the day can make the city a desert shared only geographically by many.

But even persons who have a rich family life in a busy, happy community, perhaps a life filled with service to others, need their desert experience. For the Lord has said to all and of all, "I will lead her into the desert and there I will speak to her heart." The Lord speaks by silences; he speaks his words in stillness. When he speaks words, he speaks them gently, with meanings hidden deep. Only the truly listening, only those who are a true listening, can begin to hear him.

"Human beings live not on bread alone
but on every word that comes from the mouth of God."

There are lots of hungry people in the deserts of this world, even where bread is plentiful. A human life that is nurtured only on the material level, the purely human level, is a life that suffers from a profound malnutrition. It is not a human life. In such a situation, a part of us will starve. There will be an emptiness, a frustration, a lot of unhappiness and incompletion, because the spiritual part is not being taken care of. The Christ-life is being starved.

The Christ-person that is within each one of us, that person who came into being at baptism or at the moment of original grace, needs to be fed regularly the Bread of the Word, the Words of Revelation; we need to be fed from the Sacred Scriptures. "The just person lives by faith." And "faith comes from hearing." Life begins here, with the Word of God.

Our whole life, our very being is a response to his creative word. He speaks us into being and we respond by being. He calls us out of nothingness. And his call demands a response. He is the very source of our being and life, sharing with us something of his own being and life.

And then he speaks the word of re-creation in Christ Jesus, our Lord, lifting us up from the morass that makes it virtually impossible for us to respond to him—our darkness, our weakness, our ignorance, our confusion. He speaks this Word eternally, as the Father bespeaking the Son. He expresses it first in time when the Angel Gabriel came unto the Virgin Mary. He speaks it first to most of us in the sound of waters, the waters of baptism, a wholly gratuitous gesture of love that has eternal and infinite consequence. To some it is first spoken in the silence of the heart or in the word of another that turns a heart. For each of us, it needs oft to be repeated in this way and others.

The Good Shepherd seeking the lost, the Prodigal Father welcoming home the prodigal son, the Mother Hen who would fain gather her little ones beneath her wings— in so many guises he is ever at the door knocking, knocking at the door of our hearts. He speaks through his creation, with all its wondrous seasons, its light and its dark, its cold and its hot, its storms and its gentle zephyrs. He speaks through sisters and brothers, through relatives and friends, and enemies too. He speaks through the tragedies and joys of each human life.

To those of us who have been privileged to have been called to be the daughters and sons of the Book, he speaks to us through his Sacred Scriptures. Here he speaks as friend and lover: "I no longer call you servants but friends, because I have made known to you all that the Father has made known to me." Ours are the secrets of the King.

How rich is the banquet that the Lord has laid out to fill the infinite caverns of hunger that lie within the human spirit, to feed our Christ-person, which hungers for the intimacies that belong to the Triune God. Little good does such a feast do us if we sit uncomprehending at the table, if we have eyes that see not and ears that hear not. We need to practice daily our seeing and our hearing. This we do by prayer in faith, by centering prayer, which is indeed a prayer of listening, listening with our whole being, a prayer which opens the inner eye of faith until we become keenly perceptive of the divine in every person and in all things.

"Do not put the Lord your God to the test."

The regular practice of centering prayer will have a profound effect on our lives. It will bear abundant fruit. It will not only open our eyes and our ears. It will bring about a total transformation of consciousness. But we must not test God. We must not go to our prayer looking for results. For then it will no longer be true centering prayer.

Centering prayer is a very pure prayer—pure gift, the total gift of self to God. It will bring forth fruit in our lives, the fruits of the Spirit. But we must leave all that to God. They will show up when and where and how he deems best.

If we go to centering prayer looking for results, we are still trapped within the false self, the self that is made up of what we do, what we have, and what others think of us. Our prayer becomes a "doing," something we have to do, and do right to get a certain result, to get something for the self, something *I* can grasp as *mine: "my* peace." It becomes something *I* do to please God to get what *I* want. It will no longer be the simple prayer of being, no longer the space within which the Spirit can bring forth her fruits. At best we will have the far from satisfying fruits of human doing.

Don't put God to the test. Just give. The folly of love. Love as God loves. He gets absolutely nothing out of creation; it all comes forth from him. Worship God. Serve him alone—not the self.

When we do this, the devil leaves us—our own devil, the false self. When this happens, we come to have a pure heart. We are ready to serve, to minister, to bring light to others, to be the Word of God to others.

Chapter 4

If Not a Word,
at Least a Light

Hearing that John had been arrested Jesus withdrew
to Galilee, and leaving Nazareth he went and settled
in Capernaum, beside the lake, on the borders of
Zebulum and Naphtali. This was to fulfill what was
spoken by the prophet Isaiah:

> *Land of Zebulum! Land of Naphtali!*
> *Way of the sea beyond Jordan.*
> *Galilee of the nations!*
> *The people that lived in darkness*
> *have seen a great light;*
> *on those who lived in a country of shadow dark as*
>   *death*
> *a light has dawned.*

From then onwards Jesus began his proclamation . . .

Matthew 4:12–16

When Jesus came forth from his desert experience, he entered upon his active ministry. He began to preach powerfully in word and deed.

We are led within, into the desert, not only for our own sakes but for the sake of others, for our loved ones and for all who with us form the one Christ, for all those for whom Christ lived and died. For we have been baptized into Christ, made one with him. Like him, our mission on this earth is for others.

That does not mean it is not also for ourselves, and indeed primarily for ourselves, that God our Father calls us forth and the Spirit works within us. Jesus came and lived and died for us and for our salvation. Yet who has received the greatest glory from his passion, death, and resurrection? The Lord Jesus himself. This is the wonder of our God. He wants us to live for others. He wants to use our lives for others. And yet, such is his loving plan that even as we live and labor and give ourselves for others, it is we ourselves who receive the most from it all.

Most of us, in our call to follow Jesus, will not be called to go forth to take up the life of a preacher and spend all our energies in proclaiming the good news. But we are all called to be a light enlightening those in darkness, to proclaim the good news by the way we live and are present to others, to be sacraments of God's love, expressions of that love in this world—a sign that says to all, "God loves you. You are worthy of love and respect." The compassionate way in which we respond to those who are undeserving of love will say, "Your sin and misery do not block out the divine love."

When we spend time regularly in our inner desert, letting there be space for the Spirit to do her work, she will produce in our lives those wonderful fruits of hers: love, joy, peace, patience, kindness, goodness. When we come into people's lives and are present to them, these fruits will be there. They will experience our love, our peace, our joy. And it will flow over into them if they are open to receive it. Those who are in darkness will see a great light, the light of Christ shining through us.

The last time I had breakfast with Mother Teresa in Calcutta, as I was leaving, I asked her for a "word of life" to bring to my brothers at the monastery. Mother looked at me intently, with those deep, deep brown eyes that seem to invite you into pools of embracing love. With deliberateness she spoke her words: "Father, tell them . . . to pray . . . that I *don't get in God's way.*"

A wonderful word of life. God dwells in the depths of our being, with all the fullness of his creative love. He wants to pour that love upon us, first of all in creating us ever more fully in his own image and likeness. But then through us, upon all with whom we come into contact.

There is a mysterious imperative to be found in the epistles of Saint Paul. The Holy Spirit, speaking through the Apostle to the Gentiles, tells us that "we are to fill up what is wanting in the passion of Christ." This word caused me great wonderment when I was young. (It still does, but for a different reason—because of the awesomeness of that to which we are called.) How could anything be lacking in the passion of Christ? He had died for all. He had in dying given to the Father the most perfect love and the most perfect expression of that love: "Greater love than this no man has than that he lay down his life . . ." What possibly could be lacking? What is lacking, and what we are called upon to provide, is the concrete, tangible presence of the healing power of that passion in our world and in the lives of women and men in our world today. That is our awesome responsibility.

We are to be so transparent, so pure, that the divine creative and healing love that is within us can come forth from the Christ who has made us one with him in baptism unimpeded, as a powerful presence wherever our footsteps lead us, wherever we are led by the Holy Spirit.

For most of us, our mission will be largely one of presence. To a great extent, our evangelization will be unspoken. Like the prayer itself, it will be one of being. But there is a time and place for the spoken word. A simple "God bless you" or "God is with you" to a telephone operator or at the checkout counter or toll booth can be a moment of extraordinary grace and presence. As the grace of centering prayer makes us more and more aware of the divine in others, let us reflect that sense back to them, even with words when it is appropriate. So few know how beautiful they are, how much they are loved by God.

One of the transforming moments in the life of Thomas Merton came when he was standing idly on the corner of a busy city intersection, waiting for another monk. He watched the crowds surge by without too much thought in his mind. He was more of the sensing type, just being with what is. Then, suddenly, he had a keen perception that each one of these people, and he himself too, was the beloved child of God—and none of them knew it. This perception profoundly changed Merton's life. The contemplative monk became one of the most powerful voices of the oppressed that has been raised in our century. It is still heard, even twenty years after Merton completed his journey, a great light to many a person living in darkness. His is a powerful word of light because it came from a man who knew who he truly was and continues to tell people who they truly are. The Jungian experience Merton had on the corner of Fourth and Walnut was the fruit of his hours of centering; it was the moment when what the Spirit had taught him in that prayer emerged into full consciousness.

When we ourselves have been enlightened, having opened the space by regular time spent in contemplative prayer for the Spirit to enlighten us through her gifts, then we can be present to others as a light who will enlighten their darkness simply by our presence, sometimes by our word, and always by our love.

Chapter 5

❖

Blessed Are You

Seeing the crowds, Jesus went onto the mountain.
And when he was seated his disciples came to him.
Then he began to speak. This is what he taught them:

How blessed are the poor in spirit:
the kingdom of Heaven is theirs.
Blessed are *the gentle:*
they shall have the earth as inheritance.
Blessed are those who mourn:
they shall be comforted.
Blessed are those who hunger and thirst for
    uprightness:
they shall have their fill.
Blessed are the merciful:
they shall have mercy shown them.
Blessed are the pure in heart:
they shall see God.
Blessed are the peacemakers:
they shall be recognized as the children of
    God.
Blessed are those who are persecuted in the cause
    of uprightness:
the kingdom of heaven is theirs.

Matthew 5:1–10

The redactor of Saint Matthew's Gospel, working under the inspiration of the Holy Spirit, gathered together much of the rich moral teaching of Jesus into the form of one great sermon. We usually speak of it as the Sermon on the Mount. At the beginning of this sermon we find a magnificent poetical summary of the basic attitudes that illuminate the life of the disciple and follower of Jesus Christ. We speak of these poetic sayings, or to borrow a term from the Zen Buddhist tradition, these *koans,* as the Beatitudes. They are etched deep in the mind and heart of every Christian person. We ponder them over the years. We let their wisdom ever more deeply inform our outlook and behavior. They form is us the mind and heart of Jesus Christ.

They also, in a very full and beautiful way, express the fruits of centering prayer. In centering prayer, as perhaps nowhere else so fully, we acknowledge our poverty of spirit. We let go of all our wonderful thoughts, no matter how profoundly and richly theological they might seem to be, and all our wonderful images, even though they be the richest fruit of a wonderfully endowed imagination, for we know none of these are in the least way worthy of the God whom they might seek to disclose. They can be idols as base as those workings of stone, metal, and wood worshipped by primitives. We let go of all our wonderful words, no matter how rich and beautiful the poetic mat into which they have been woven. We let go of our feelings and emotions, whatever their intensity or vibrancy. In short, we let go of all the products of our own poor spirit and content ourselves, as Abba Isaac counseled John Cassian, with the poverty of a single word, a God-given word —a word that doesn't try to represent the God of infinite love or try to represent our sentiments toward him, but that simply points toward him, that directs the gift of our being to him. In our poverty we give him all that we have to give—not our thoughts or feelings or aspirations, but simply our very selves. And we know it is a poor enough gift. But it is all that we have. We give it to him. It is his.

And a wonderful thing happens. When we leave behind the realm of our feelings and our thoughts and our images, of all our doings and havings, we discover that there is deep within us, at the center, the very kingdom of God. We are his. When we fully acknowledge this and hand ourselves over to him in this prayer of being, we discover that reciprocally he is ours. We discover in this prayer that, indeed, the kingdom of heaven is within and that it is ours, for we are one with its king. All that we are is his. And all that is his is ours.

Gentleness is one of the fruits of the Holy Spirit enumerated by Saint Paul in the fifth chapter of his letter to the Galatians. It arises in us out of the experience of being held so gently yet so completely and powerfully in the embrace of divine creative love. It comes from our knowing our oneness with all created beings in the center that is God. As we rest in the center, we come to know that we are indeed one with all and we hold all in the gentle all-embracing love that is God, the Holy Spirit, who has been given to us as our spirit.

Popular is the image of the poor man of Assisi, Francis by name. Out of his contemplative experience he spoke to Sister Moon and Brother Sun. All the animal kingdom seemed to respond to his gentle hospitality. He knew his oneness with them, and they, in turn, sensed the safety and warmth of his gentleness. The whole earth was indeed his inheritance.

I had a wonderful friend—I still do, though he is in the kingdom of heaven now. He was a warm and witty Irishman by the name of Jeremiah F. O'Sullivan. He was the father of Cistercian studies in America, a much-loved teacher, revered by all his students and colleagues. Each morning, after he saluted his sovereign Lord, Jerry would go out to the garden to salute his beloved plants. He would walk among them solicitous of their needs, singing gently to them of their beauty. The plants generously rewarded this gentle love with some of the largest beets, cabbages, and carrots I have ever seen. Among Jerry's parting wishes was that on the way to the cemetery he could pass one final time among his beloved plants. And this he did with some two hundred cars of mourners—or should I say celebrants—accompanying him. It was a little bit of the earth that Jerry inherited there, but in truth it was the whole of it, for it filled every cranny of his being with a simple, radiant joy.

There is great comfort to be found in centering prayer. We mourn our sins, perhaps more than most, when we center, for we see them so clearly in the light of the divine presence. We see their heinousness in the light of such an immensity of goodness and mercy. Yet, at the very same moment, we know the totality of the forgiveness that is ours. We are comforted.

We mourn the evils of all the world. Knowing our oneness with all things, their pain, their sin, their grief are ours. Yet we find the comfort of hope. The God of all comfort is with us. Where sin abounds, grace abounds yet more. We have a saviour, and he has already saved us. All is taken care of. We have a healer. All our wounds will be healed. We have a risen Lord; he has overcome death. And we, too, shall arise. And there will be a new heaven and a new earth. Even as we mourn, we are brought into the knowledge of all this and we are comforted.

In our mourning, we hunger and thirst for the healing and wholing of all. As we experience the goodness and wholeness of God, we hunger and thirst for this for all. And, at the same time, we know that God has all in his loving hold: he's got the whole wide world in his hands. His ways are not our ways, nor his thoughts our thoughts. They are far beyond us, yet we are filled with assurance that in the end, for those who love God, all things will work together unto good. For we know this God who is love and power and the source of all that is.

And knowing our oneness with all, as well as knowing our own poverty, our sinfulness, our misery, how can we not be merciful. What mother will not have mercy on the child of her womb because it is the child of her womb— flesh of her flesh, bone of her bone, enlivened by her very own blood. Yet, in an age when millions of mothers are so unnatural as to cast out the children of their own wombs, we come in centering to know that the oneness we have with each and every fellow human is even more bonding than the natural ties of flesh and blood. Our oneness is in the sharing of divine being. And when we see that divine being desecrated in any being, the wellsprings of our mercy are opened and mercy from the Source of all mercy pours through us. We obtain not only all the mercy we need but a superabundance to pour out on our needy sisters and brothers.

Forgiveness is far more than giving. It does not just give what is due or what is beyond what is due. It gives unto folly. It gives back to an offender the gift of his dignity and our friendship without exacting any retribution. We have been told to pray "Forgive us as we forgive." We have been taught that this is the way of the Lord. He only forgives to the measure we have forgiven. In centering prayer, where we learn our intimate oneness with our offending brother and sister, we are convicted by the folly of any unforgiveness, we enter into full forgiveness, we are totally forgiven. This is the mercy of God.

With this, we are well on the way to becoming pure in heart, something that is fully achieved only in the death of the false self. As we let go of the false self, that construct that we have created—and greatly been aided by others in the creating—out of what we think we have, what we imagine we are accomplishing and what images of ourselves we project upon others, we escape all illusion. Finally, we come to stand naked before God and see ourselves reflected back to ourselves in his all-loving eyes and discover in our nakedness and truth that we are an incredibly beautiful image of God, his beloved. Lying completely open to him and the gaze of his creative love, we are totally cleansed. As our vision is cleared, the inner eye of our faith is opened and illumined by the activity of the Holy Spirit through her gifts. We see God. We know in whom we believe. We see God in himself in faith. We see God in ourselves, his beautiful image. We see God in others. We see God in all the creation.

The Latin name for the Spirit's gift of understanding is *intellectus,* derived from *inter,* within, and *legere,* to read.

We read what is within. We see God within everyone and everything, as the creative source of all. Or to take it from the English, we see what "stands under," the gift of understanding.

Centering prayer makes us peacemakers of our very nature. Our own deep peacefulness, the harmony of order in our lives, spreads out among those with whom we live, those whom we serve.

It has never ceased to amaze me, and seems a bit of a miracle, that the Nobel Peace Prize was awarded to Mother Teresa of Calcutta. Not that I do not see her as a tremendous woman of peace—one has but to look into her eyes to see and experience great mercy, care, and peacefulness—and a powerful agent of peace in this world of ours. What amazes me is that the committee which has bestowed that coveted prize on so many political machinators was able to recognize what a true force for peace a contemplative person like Mother Teresa is. Such peacemakers are more readily recognized as the children of God, but are not so readily recognized by the powers of this world as the true sources of world peace. Such peacemakers might more readily be persecuted by the powers of this world as they labor in the cause of uprightness.

However, the one who practices centering prayer does not wait around for others to come along and persecute them so that they can attain the kingdom of heaven. They set about persecuting themselves—their false selves—so that they can be free of the tyranny of their own thoughts and feelings, of their own interpretations of reality, of the defensiveness and competitiveness that closes them in on themselves. Freed from all of this they can be open to Reality, to the wonderfully affirming presence of God within them, their sure defense—to the kingdom of God within as their kingdom.

And, of course, living in this way, we can be sure that we will possess the kingdom of God as our own kingdom *forever.*

Chapter 6

❖

Children of Our Father

But I say this to you, love your enemies, and pray for those who persecute you, so that you may be children of your Father in heaven, for he causes his sun to rise on the bad as well as the good, and sends down rain to fall on the upright and the wicked alike.

Matthew 5:44–45

When I was in the college seminary, I took a course entitled Ascetical and Mystical Theology. It was supposed to show us the way to become saints. We spent the entire year on the first part of the textbook, exploring all the vices we had to get rid of, all the temptations we had to overcome, and all the virtues we had to acquire. In a state of mental exhaustion (I didn't really try to do all these things; I just tried to learn about them) we arrived at the last day of class and the second section of the book: mystical theology. Here the good father who was teaching the course dramatically closed the book, stating, "This part of the book will be of little concern to you unless you are one of those rare persons who lives to a great old age and has years of retirement to work at it. If you are appointed chaplain to the Carmelites—then you will have to get it out and study it."

This was indeed sad. And for more than one reason. It reinforced the then-popular idea that contemplative prayer was some very rare commodity which, in the ordinary course of events, in no wise belonged to those priests and religious dedicated to the active ministry and certainly not to the simple faithful. Moreover, the exhausting journey through the first part of the book definitely inculcated the idea that the "spiritual" life was a long, hard ordeal and few are those who have the courage, tenacity, and strength to get very far in it. It was a great project and only the most hearty dare undertake it with any seriousness. The rest of us would have enough to do getting through our daily duties without grievous sin.

I had heard of those athletes of old, the fathers of the desert, who sought to outdo each other in their austerities, undertaking incredible penances and fasting beyond what seemed possible to the human. I recalled with better humor those delightful vignettes in Saint Bernard's *Steps of Humility.* The humble abbot of Clairvaux tells us he is better prepared to describe the descending steps of pride than their opposite and then goes on to depict, among others, the proud monk, darting glances around the refectory to make sure no one is eating less than he.

The pernicious thing about making the quest for holiness a project is precisely that: it becomes a project of the false self. Something we are accomplishing. So, instead of dying to self, the false self, we are rather building it up by all our accomplishments at eradicating vice and cultivating virtue. We are "acquiring" virtues, one more collection of things that the false self can use to build itself up.

The only way to true holiness, Christian holiness, is to die to the false self—the self that is made up of what we do and what we have and what we think others think of us—so that the true self, that beautiful image of God that ever comes forth from his creative love, and not from our efforts, can emerge.

This is precisely what we do in centering prayer. There is no project in centering prayer for us to accomplish. Rather, we demolish the false self in the most effective way possible: by simply ignoring it, with all its clamors and eagerness to do. When we struggle with someone, we at least acknowledge that they are worth struggling with. But when we totally ignore them, they virtually cease to exist as far as we are concerned. In centering prayer there is no struggle. We simply turn to God, thus ignoring the false self. And each time it does succeed in catching our attention, we simply, gently return to the Lord, using our prayer word, turning our back on the false self in turning to him.

The false self very much likes to make a project out of things, make them hard, and make sure we are doing them right so that it can then pat itself on the back for doing such a good job. There is no place for this in centering prayer. Like little children, we simply jump into our Father's arms and let him do the rest. There is no cause to pat ourselves on the back. Who can pat himself on the back for resting in the arms of the one he loves?

But this false self never ceases trying to get into the act. If it can do nothing else, it will try to make something of the prayer word. The anonymous author of *The Cloud of Unknowing* has sage advice for us here: "If your mind begins to intellectualize over the meaning and connotations of this little word, remind yourself that its value lies in its simplicity. Do this and I assure you these thoughts will vanish."

Many succumb to the temptation to make more of a project out of the centering prayer by adding to the method. Most people do find some little preparation helps them to get into the prayer. Unfortunately, they incorporate this into the teaching as they hand it on. The next person adds a little more: a little breathing, a little stretching, a little count down, some imaging, and so on. There is one author who asserts that it is better to meditate for one hour once a day rather than for a half hour twice a day. When you look at the method as he presents it, you see why. He has added so much to it that it takes almost a half hour to get into it!

Once I was sharing the centering prayer at a center near Washington, D.C. The center offered programs for those who were having difficulty with drugs and alcohol, among other things. It found the centering prayer a very great help to them and incorporated the prayer as a regular part of the program. As I was leaving, I was presented with a large framed picture (which I had to carry through New York on the way home). It depicted two animals—seals, I think—nose to nose. Over them was the caption K.I.S.S., for Keep It Simple, Sweety, an excellent motto for centering prayer.

Jesus tells us in the words from the Sermon on the Mount his way to holiness. We are to be like our heavenly Father. A chip off the old block, if I may dare put it so profanely. It is a way, not of acquiring virtues, of slaying vices. It is the way of compassionate love. The Father lets his "sun" and his "rain," his favor and his grace, come down upon good and bad alike, on the just and the unjust —namely, upon all. It is a way of simple, gentle love. And it is in centering prayer we learn how to do this—how to abide in simple gentle love, letting all the rest go by, all those assessments, thoughts, and feelings that make it so difficult for us to simply love.

Centering prayer helps us in another way in this way of compassionate love. It is through centering prayer that we open the space for the Holy Spirit to begin to act in us through his gifts. We gain a new perception, one that enables us to see what is beneath the surface. We begin to perceive in each person that which is of God in them, his beautiful image. We see each one, no matter how foolishly he or she may have acted, as the child beloved of the Father for whom he sent his Son to die. Spontaneously there begins to come to our lips the prayer of our Master: "Father, forgive them. They do not know what they are doing." We wish them well and pray for them.

Even enemies? Those who have deeply hurt us or, worse, have hurt those whom we love? That is what Jesus calls us to here. And, yes, as our godlike perception grows, through centering prayer, we see what Jesus sees in us sinners, someone beautiful enough to die for.

In truth, this does not come easy. And it does not come of ourselves. Corrie ten Boom has told us a powerful story. This good Dutch Christian suffered much in the German concentration camps for having helped save Jews. She suffered most from witnessing the sufferings and eventual death of her sister. After the war she traveled widely, preaching forgiveness. Then one day, at the end of just such a talk, a man whom she recognized came up to thank

her. He told her how much her talk on forgiveness had
heartened him. Corrie recognized him as the guard in the
camp who had been so brutal and caused them so much
suffering. When he extended his hand to Corrie, she
found her hand glued to her side. She could not bring
herself to raise it to accept his. Her heart was torn. She
sent an anguished prayer to the Lord. But she could not
bring herself to raise her hand and accept his. Then her
spirit cried to the Lord, Give me your forgiveness for him.
And a power flowed through her into her arm, and her
hand went out to warmly embrace the other.

Sometimes it is beyond us. But centering prayer teaches
us that it need not, and ultimately does not, come from us.
All of the divine creative energy resides within us at the
center of our being. It is his power and his love, his sun
and his rain, that can always come forth from us for the
just and the unjust, the friend and the enemy. Even with
the friend it will be something far fuller, more satisfying,
and more worthy of our friendship when it flows directly
from the divine source.

We have already shared Mother Teresa's good word, a
true word of life. In centering prayer we learn to get out of
God's way. So that we can indeed be true children of our
Father, acting just like him, being to others just like him,
for it will be his life and his love, his sun and his rain, that
will be flowing through us.

Chapter 7

❖

Being All There

But when you give alms, your left hand must not
know what your right hand is doing; your alms giving
must be secret, and your Father who sees all that is
done in secret will reward you.

Matthew 6:3–4

"Your left hand must not know what your right hand is
doing." Or we might say, your left eye should not be
watching what your right eye is about. For we are quite the
experts at keeping an eye on ourselves. When Judgment
Day comes, the Lord is not going to have to have a prose-
cuting attorney. We have been keeping a pretty good eye
on ourselves and will be able to give a full report.

We do tend to live with a divided consciousness, broken into two subjects—one that is acting and another that
is watching the acting subject, treating it as an object. We
thus find ourselves alienated from ourselves and suffer
from this self-alienation. Instead of being all there, with
both eyes on what we are doing, giving it our whole attention, we tend to have one eye on what we are doing and

the other eye on ourselves doing it. And this other eye tends to be a very judgmental eye, depriving us of much of the simple joy that can be found in doing what we are doing. This not only dissipates our presence, it also builds up the false self.

Obviously, if we are keeping one eye on ourselves, taking note of what we are doing, evaluating it, fitting it in with our past and future, concerned with how we look and what we are getting out of what we are doing, a great deal of the attention and energy that could have gone into what we are about is being siphoned off.

How often, when we are talking with someone, do we have both eyes on our interlocutor, literally and metaphorically? Usually we are looking around, at least part of the time, not wanting to miss out on the other things that are going on around us. At the same time, our mind is watching our performance, judging the performance of the other, making comparisons, exploring alien ideas, thinking about what is coming next or what has already transpired, and so on. The person who is speaking with us, of course, perceives this, consciously or unconsciously, and is often engaged in a similar way. As a result, he or she feels the need to repeat what they are trying to communicate, striving to gain fuller attention and comprehension amid the competing ocular and mental wanderings. With all this static, much less true communication is achieved in much more time.

The most pernicious element in all of this, and the most prevalent, is our need to look good. Do we do anything that is not in some way influenced or motivated by our need to look good? Just think over some of the things you have done in the last hour or so and see how this came into play. This happens even when we are doing something completely on our own, for the person we most need to convince that we are looking good is ourselves. This is the way we build up our false self, the self that is made up of what we do, what we have, and what others think of us.

And this is precisely what our Lord is taking aim at here: doing things to look good, not only so that we might look good to others but also to build up our smug self-satisfaction. Our whole being should be so engaged in the good we are doing that there is no possibility of part of us watching ourselves and feeding on self.

Centering prayer is a great school where we learn to do precisely this. In faith and love we simply be to the Lord. We are all there to him. And whenever we become aware of ourselves, what we are doing, how we are performing, and the like, we gently turn back to the Lord, putting both eyes on him. Gradually we learn how to be all there, to keep both eyes on what we are about and not one eye there and one eye on ourselves. To grow in this ability is, of course, not the aim of centering prayer. The only aim is God, to be to God. And the way of the practice is to keep both eyes on him, gently using our love word to do this. But it is one of the effects of being faithful to the practice of centering prayer that we grow in our ability, under God's grace, to be all there, not only during our centering but in all the other areas of our lives.

As this ability grows, it flows over into our other activities. Especially is this so as the activity of the Holy Spirit through the gifts grows in each one of our lives. We become more and more aware of the presence of God not only in the persons with whom we communicate but also in all the energies that we are using in our various endeavors. And as our love for him and desire to be one with him grows, we want to be all there where we are encountering him at this moment.

My first spiritual father used to say, "The past and the future are just other forms of self; God is now." We want to be fully present to what is right now—for here is where life and reality and God are—rather than evaluating what is already slipping into the past.

Saint John Cassian, in his "First Conference," tells us the aim of the Christian life, with all its ascesis, is to attain purity of heart. This is just another way, a more classical way, of saying that the aim of the Christian life is to learn to be all there, no longer treating ourselves partially as an object and trying to get that object-self to look good. No, we are just all there—for God, with God, in God. Quite simply, we let God be our all: "My God and my All." As the fathers would say, *Age quod agis:* Do what you are doing. Or as our Master says here, "Your left hand must not know what your right hand is doing."

When we act in this way, when we are all there, what we do is indeed done in secret. It is hidden even from ourselves. The gift is total; it is a total gift of self. We are totally in the giving, totally to the other. This is the stuff of ecstasy.

Chapter 8

✥

Do Not Babble . . .
Your Father Knows

And when you pray, do not imitate the hypocrites: they love to say their prayers standing up in the synagogues and at the street corners for people to see them. In truth I tell you, they have had their reward. But when you pray, *go to your private room,* shut yourself in, and so pray to your Father who is in that secret place, and your Father who sees all· that is done in secret will reward you.

In your prayers do not babble as the gentiles do, for they think that by using many words they will make themselves heard. Do not be like them; your Father knows what you need before you ask him. So you should pray like this:

> Our Father in heaven,
> may your name be held holy,
> your kingdom come,
> your will be done,
> on earth as in heaven.
> Give us today our daily bread.

And forgive us our debts,
as we have forgiven those who are in debt to us.
And do not put us to the test,
but save us from the Evil One.

Matthew 6:5–13

The fathers of the Church and the whole tradition have told us that when we listen to Sacred Scripture, if we want to hear all that God has to say to us, we need to approach the Word with different listenings.

Most fundamentally there is the literal or historical sense of Scripture—precisely what the words are saying, what the author is recounting. This is the foundation of all the other meanings of Sacred Scripture. It is not always easy to obtain. Herein lies the extensive labors of the scholars, who must study the languages used in the Sacred Texts, their contemporary meanings, the historical contexts, the literary forms, and many other things. When we are seeking to enter fully into the literal meaning of the text, commentaries and study groups can be a great help.

Besides this literal sense of Scripture, there are a number of what the fathers call spiritual senses. In perceiving the presence of these, they are led by the same Holy Spirit who inspired the text and the sacred writers. Saint Paul, writing under inspiration, spoke of these deeper meanings in Galatians 4:24–26:

There is an allegory here: these women stand for the two covenants. The one given on Mount Sinai—that is Hagar, whose children are born into slavery; now Sinai is a mountain in Arabia and represents Jerusalem in its present state, for she is in slavery together with her children. But the Jerusalem above is free, and that is the one that is our mother.

We can see here Saint Paul takes the historical story of Sarah and Hagar, of Isaac and Ishmael, and finds in it deeper meanings related to the fuller revelation that has come. Jerusalem itself is given a spiritual meaning, as is Mount Sinai. In the reading of the Old Testament, Paul finds a deeper understanding of the new and of the life we are called to by that new covenant.

Another example from Paul is in 1 Corinthians 10:2–4, 11:

> In the cloud and in the sea they were all baptized into Moses; all ate the same spiritual food and all drank the same spiritual drink, since they drank from the spiritual rock which followed them, and that rock was Christ . . . Now all these things happened to them by way of example, and they were described in writing to be a lesson for us, to whom it has fallen to live in the last days of the ages.

The fathers distinguish among three spiritual senses: (1) the *allegorical sense,* or the mystery hidden within the literal meaning, as when Paul finds within the interaction of Sarah and Hagar the interaction between the new and old dispensations, (2) the *moral sense,* the response to which the literal sense calls us, or how we are to live the teaching of the Scriptures, and (3) the *anagogic* or *unitive sense* of the Sacred Word, that toward which all the others tend.

Thus, for example, we might read of Jerusalem. The

literal and historical sense of this word speaks of a city on Mount Sion, the sacred city, the kingly city of David, the city where our Saviour shed his blood for us. Morally, Jerusalem might be heard as the call of grace for us all to belong to the Church, the kingdom of God on earth, with a true and obedient allegiance. Allegorically or mystically, Jerusalem is the Church. And ultimately it is the realization of the salvific mission of the Lord when the new Jerusalem descends from heaven, a bride adorned and ready for complete union with the Divine Bridegroom (Rv 21:2).

With this kind of hearing, let us now return to our present text. We are told that when we pray, we should literally go to our private room, shut ourselves in, and pray to our Father, who is in that secret place. This is good practical advice for anyone hoping to live a serious prayer life that will lead to deeper union with the Father in Christ.

But we can hear a deeper meaning in this. Our most private room is that deep place within us, what we have been calling our "center." There, indeed, our Father dwells. And we are invited to go to that center, shut out all else and abide there with our Father in prayer. This is precisely what we do in centering prayer. With the use of our prayer word, we, as it were, close the door, or to use another image, we create a cloud of unknowing, leaving everything outside and ourselves quietly and peacefully within with the Father.

While we are there, we do not need to babble, to repeat constantly our word as some sort of mantra. Nor do we need to use many words. One simple word is enough. And even that can slip away as we abide in the silence with our

Father. We do not need words. We need simply to be with him. He knows and understands all. He will take care of all.

Did you ever notice in the Gospels how those two great women of prayer Mary the Mother of Jesus and Mary of Bethany obtained from the Lord his first and his greatest miracles without asking. They simply let the concern of their hearts be there before Jesus—"They have no wine. He who you love is sick"—knowing that he would take care of everything. Which he did.

We monks often marvel at the wonderful way in which our Lord takes care of our families and loved ones. It is not that we are constantly talking to him about them. It is just that while we are centering, resting with him in contemplative prayer, he sees our special love for those he has given to us, and in his love for us, he embraces them with a special love of his own. We can count on him.

Surely we will still want at times to pray quite specifically, especially when we are gathered with others and seeking to be one with them in their concerns and needs. Indeed, spontaneously all through the day we will be speaking to the Lord, at times praising and thanking him, at other times asking him to help us or to take care of particular situations.

But when we go to the center, it is time to let all that go and simply rest with him, knowing that our Father knows what we need before we ask him.

All this being so, there is nonetheless a value in allowing the deep experience of prayer which we have in the centering to rise to a more conscious level. Our Lord has given us a formula of prayer which we use at the end of our time of restful contemplation. If we allow the words and phrases of the Lord's Prayer to quietly arise and expand in the period after our centering, we will discover that the Lord has, in fact, not just given us a formula of prayer to be repeated by rote. Rather, he has given us in these brief but pregnant phrases a whole school of prayer, indeed, a school of life. They are, in themselves, under the action of the Holy Spirit, able to teach us all there is to be learned about living the life of Christ, that life into which we have been baptized.

Chapter 9

❖

Coming into the Light

> The lamp of the body is the eye. It follows that if your
> eye is clear, your whole body will be filled with light.
> But if your eye is diseased, your whole body will be
> darkness. If then, the light inside you is darkened,
> what darkness that will be.
>
> *Matthew 6:22–23*

Through the centuries there have been many theories
about how the human eye works. Today, with modern
physiology, we have some certain knowledge, though we
still have our questions and are confronted with some
mystery.

I do not know what was the prevalent theory of seeing
in our Lord's time. At one time it was commonly thought
that we are able to see because a light goes out from the
eye to the object perceived. This is perhaps the theory that
influences Jesus' analogy here. Or he might have something much simpler in mind, just the question of a clean
window or a clear opening in the wall that serves as such.
If the opening or window is clear, sunlight floods in and

the room inside is bright and cheerful. The occupants can easily see things, including themselves. If the window is covered with soil or the opening obscured by vines and bushes, then little light will penetrate. The room inside will always remain dark, no matter how much sunlight is pouring down upon it. If the opening is totally covered, it will be completely dark within and those inside will not be able to see anything.

Eye disease often takes the form of some kind of film clouding the surface of the eye and affecting the sight of the victim, making even the brightest day seem dull and dark. The darkness is experienced within. The condition of the day outside has little effect upon it. If one is working from the theory that sight is caused by some light source within the eye, then the disease is seen as affecting this light source and causing the experience of darkness. This light source being darkened, the person will be permanently in the dark, no matter what alterations of light there may be outside.

Our Lord, of course, is not here concerned with eyes and eyesight, physical light and dark. His concern lies with the inner eye, the eye of the soul, the human intellect. And that special lamp that has been given to it, the lamp that is illumined by the light of faith so that we can perceive the things of God.

Our eye, indeed, has lost its clarity. When the soul itself became diseased, the eye was affected. A certain darkness of mind is one of the effects of original sin, a darkness which is enhanced by the influences of the whole sinful environment into which we are born. Thoughts and images whirl about. Half-truths and lies, the fantasies of an ill-controlled and overfed imagination create a distracting kaleidoscope. The steam of passion further clouds the inner eye and distorts its vision. If the light of faith is totally extinguished, *what darkness that will be.*

It is so dark that the person is usually totally unaware of his darkness, his ignorance of the things of faith, of the things he most needs to know to understand himself and find the happiness he is so futilely seeking. We know what we know, and it is little enough. And we know what we know we don't know. And that is a good bit more. But then there are those vast realms of knowledge which we don't even know we don't know.

We are each a certain seeing or hearing or listening, if you will. We have a certain scope of perception to take in what is to be perceived, whether it be presented by sight or sound or taste or touch or smell. Our listening or seeing has been formed by our life experiences. The perimeters are narrow enough. We all tend to be limited by certain prejudices. But we have all been endowed with a mind that has, as it were, an infinite capacity. If it has not been too dulled (as it can be by drugs, liquor, or sex), when something is perceived that reaches beyond the established perimeters and if they are not held rigidly in place by prejudice, they expand and we arrive at a greater listening or seeing.

In centering prayer we drop all our perimeters. We let go of all our limited and limiting thoughts and images and sit in the silence wide open to Reality. The only limit is the limitless questing of a mind that has been made in the image of God and has a capacity for the infinite Truth that is God.

There can be a natural contemplation. A wonderful natural perception of God perceived through his creation and, above all, through the wonder of our own being. However, the light of faith greatly enhances our vision. Through it, we are opened to that knowledge that comes only through the revelation, through knowledge of the inmost realities of God: "I no longer call you servants but friends, because I have made known to you all the things the Father has made known to me."

And there is yet a greater light still. As that great Doctor of the Church Saint Thomas Aquinas says, "Where the mind leaves off the heart goes beyond." There is love-knowledge, the ineffable perceptions of love, brought about in this case by the Holy Spirit, who is the very Love of God, present within us and operating through those special faculties we received at baptism called the gifts of the Holy Spirit.

A great healing takes place in centering prayer. All the disease of passion and emotion, of dark and crippling memories, does not long withstand the light that is flooding in, or rather the light that is flowing forth from the Infinite Source that is within. This is a sad reality: the infinite all-healing Light is already present within each one of us and is always present. But as long as we cling to the limiting darkening of our own little thoughts and images and feelings and emotions, that great Light is hardly perceived and can little exercise its healing powers.

It is only when we are willing to let go of our own thoughts and images and sit in the full openness of trusting love that the Divine Light can fully enter into all the recesses of our soul and work its total healing. This Light is so great, so beyond us, that the initial effect is that of darkness. We seem to sit there completely in the dark. But the Light is doing its work. The inner eye is gradually being healed and opening to the deifying Light which will enable it to see all reality as it truly is.

Have you ever had the experience of attending an afternoon movie on a bright, sunny day. For an hour or two you sit in a dark theater, completely taken up with the light cast on the wall (a light so weak that all other light has to be virtually eliminated so that you can perceive it), with a superficial reality, a product of our own creation. It grasps you as though it were indeed reality. You laugh and weep and experience all sorts of emotions. Then the show ends and you step out into the full sunlight. What is your first experience? For a moment everything is black. The light is too strong for your eyes, or at least for what your eyes have become accustomed to. It takes a bit of time for them to adjust. Then, under the powerful light of the sun, you begin to see things as they really are.

Until we begin to open our inner eye through the practice of centering prayer or contemplation, we will perceive our own thoughts and images as reality and be wholly taken up with them. We have sat in this theater of life for how many years? When we begin to practice centering prayer, we step out into the light of the Son, the Divine Light. At first, indeed, all is dark, very dark. The deifying Light is infinitely beyond that to which we have so long been accustomed. It takes time for the inner eye to adjust. We are sitting in darkness, or so it seems. We are actually sitting in an overwhelming Light. Only gradually, under the gentle operation of the Holy Spirit, through the gifts, does our inner eye begin to perceive reality as it truly is. Then even our thoughts and images, which for so long have been removed from true presence and by that removal rendered quite lifeless, are reconnected with their life-giving source and have a new clarity about them, one that enables us to share them in a way that engenders experience and brings about presence. This is the source of the great power of a true poet or evangelizer.

One of the things that makes centering prayer so difficult is that it puts us in touch with our own darkness. As we sit there, we become accutely aware of how much we do need the deifying Light. It is not easy to sit in the darkness waiting for the Light to work its healing effect, removing the disease that clouds the inner eye. This may take what seems to us a very long time. Unfortunately, it has been for years and years we have operated with diseased eyes, always increasing the disease and its darkening effect. It may well take years for all the needed healing to take place.

God, of course, could—as Jesus so often did when he walked this earth—effect an instantaneous and complete healing. He does sometimes in the first days of our centering give us moments of great light. He is consoling a weak one, encouraging us to continue on. But usually, in his love he wants us to have the merit and joy of being a part of the healing. So he leaves us sitting there to go through the gradual process with the Divine Healer.

Almost without our perceiving it, the healing takes place. Remember the parable of the seed sown which quietly germinated, sprouted, and grew while the farmer went about his daily chores and enjoyed his night's rest. As we pursue our centering practice, we go about our daily Christian living and twice a day or more we take our rest in the center. Indeed, it might seem at times as if we were but sleeping. That was the experience of no less a prayer than Saint Teresa of Jesus, the great spiritual mother of

Ávila. But the activity of the Spirit is going on and the fruits of the Spirit are growing in our lives. Oftentimes, others are more aware of them than we. This is one of the reasons why it is always good to have a companion on the journey—a spiritual father or a spiritual mother, a soul friend or a guru, or whatever you wish to call him or her. This friend can encourage us by what he or she perceives.

Perseverance is the important thing. Fidelity to practice. Only in this way can a complete healing come about, can all the disease be removed. Then, when that inner eye is clear, our whole life will be filled with light.

Chapter 10

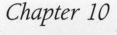

Him First

That is why I am telling you not to worry about your life and what you are to eat, nor about your body and what you are to wear. Surely life is more than food, and the body more than clothing! Look at the birds of the sky. They do not sow or reap or gather into barns, yet your heavenly Father feeds them. Are you not worth much more than they are? Can any of you, no matter how much you worry, add one single cubit to your span of life? And why worry about clothing? Think of the flowers growing in the fields; they never have to work or spin; yet I assure you that not even Solomon in all his royal robes was clothed like one of these. Now if that is how God clothes the wild flowers growing in the field which are there today and thrown into the furnace tomorrow, will he not much more look after you, you who have so little faith? So do not worry: do not say, "What are we to eat? What are we to drink? What are we to wear? It is the gentiles who set their hearts on all these things. Your heavenly Father knows you need them all. Set your hearts on his kingdom first, and on God's saving justice, and all these other things will be given you as well. So do not worry about tomorrow: tomorrow will take care of itself. Each day has enough trouble of its own.

Matthew 6:25–34

As we have already noted a number of times, the false self is constituted basically of our identifying with what we have, what we do, and what other people think of us. I am nobody until I have the big house or the big car or the fancy clothes, until I can get a book published or become a big shot in my organization, until enough people sit up and take note of me. The more they do, the more I am.

This false identification is something that is almost inevitably inculcated by our present society. If family and friends who have a primary formative influence on us are not infected by it—and there are very few who are not— the advertising media, including television, press, and larger-than-life billboards, do everything they possibly can to make us think this way.

We speak of a "transformation" of consciousness. Our consciousness has a certain form, a certain way in which we hold things and life itself. The false self is our form of consciousness. We see ourselves, and hold ourselves, as being what we have, what we do, what others think of us. And we see everything and everyone else in relation to this. The things I possess have value insofar as they serve this false self, build it up, make others think better of me, and make me think better of myself. (However, in our more honest moments, we see through this.) And this is equally true of the things I do. Much of the time we see others as competitors—competing to have the same things or better, to accomplish greater things, and generally trying to upstage us and get the more affirming approval from others. At the same time, we see others as important sources of our being, for in our own eyes we exist to the extent that we exist and loom large and worthwhile in the eyes of others. How much of our energy is expended on looking good! How much potentially powerful creativity is short-circuited out of the fear of how in fact we will look if we dare to be creative and innovative. The false self as a dominating mind-set is very enslaving.

What our Lord sets forth here is diametrically opposite to the false self. He calls for a new form of consciousness, a new way of looking at things and holding them, a transformation of consciousness. He is speaking to generally quite poor people who live in what we would consider rather primitive circumstances, so he stays very much with the basics. The poor unfortunately are not automatically freed from the false self, only the poor in spirit are. One can be very poor and not poor in spirit, just as one can be very rich and be truly poor in spirit. Though the really poor, who have to live from hand to mouth, have a much better chance of being poor in spirit and have a lot less potential to build up the false self.

We have life, we have a body that is enlivened by that life. These are the gratuitous gifts of God. Herein lies our essential greatness, for herein lies the very image of God and participation in his own life and being. Our minimal needs are not to be denied, but struggling for self-aggrandizement is not going to build us up—really.

Our Lord is actually bringing out three things here, each of which we learn and experience in centering prayer.

The first is that God is the Source. All our worrying, fretting, planning, doing, and acquiring are ultimately not going to make the difference. We can't add one single cubit to the span of our lives. In centering prayer we get in touch with God at the very center of our being, the ground of our being, as the Source. We come to know our true self as that beautiful person who at each moment comes forth from his creative love. It isn't what we do or what we have or what others think of us that makes us. We are. On the contrary, instead of our being created by our doings and havings, with God we are the creative source that does whatever we want—"I can do all things in him who strengthens me."—and have whatever we want—"Ask and you shall receive."

Incidentally, note that Jesus uses an interesting metaphor here. We usually think of life in terms of time. But he uses the metaphor of space: "cubit" and "span." For him who sees things in terms of the eternal "now," duration is not the important thing. It is not the duration of our life span that matters, but the bigness of life, the quality of life. We are, or become, more concerned about the duration or prolongation of life to the extent that we experience a lack of fullness and fulfillment in our lives. When our lives are full of God, we know his presence and love; then we have little concern about the time of our transition to the heavenly life.

Centering prayer puts us in touch with God not only as the Source but as a source who is immediately present to us and has a constant care and love for us. At every moment, he is bringing us forth from his very own being, sharing his being, goodness, and truth with us. (I am not postulating pantheism here. There is a very real distinction between his essential being which always was and is and will be and our participation in his being which began at a particular point in time—even though it was always present in him in his eternal "now"—and is now and always will be.) There is not a moment when he is not "thinking" of us, caring for us. Surely then, we can fully rely on him to provide for all our needs according as is best for us, remembering always these salutary words of his: "My thoughts are not your thoughts, nor your ways my ways, but as high as is heaven above earth so are my thoughts beyond your thoughts and my ways beyond your ways." Our heavenly Father knows all our needs and he will take care of them in the way that is best for us *if we let him.*

This is the third point that our Lord makes here and that we practice in centering prayer: "Set your hearts on his kingdom first, and on God's saving justice, and all these other things will be given you as well." God wants to give us everything we need and more, not only for body but also for spirit. But he respects us; he reverences our freedom. He won't force anything on us. If we want to try to do it on our own, he will let us, with the due consequences (seen so graphically in the lives of so many of our brothers and sisters who have chosen this option). He will come into our lives and act in them, caring for us and enriching us in every way, only to the extent we open to him. In centering prayer we open to God; we seek to open to him totally, so there are absolutely no obstacles to his doing all he wants in our lives. As we continue in our centering practice, we unmask more and more the false self and let it wither as we discover more and more the true self. We do come to set our hearts on the Lord and on his kingdom *first,* knowing that all these other things will be given us as well.

The purity of heart, abandonment, and trust that our Lord is calling his disciples to here is learned and lived in the daily practice of centering prayer. And through that practice, it becomes the prevailing attitude during the rest of our life.

Chapter 11

Known by the Fruits

You will be able to tell them by their fruits. Can
people pick grapes from thorns, or figs from thistles.
In the same way, a sound tree produces good fruit
but a rotten tree bad fruit. A sound tree cannot bear
bad fruit, nor a rotten tree bear good fruit. Any tree
that does not produce good fruit is cut down and
thrown on the fire. I repeat, you will be able to tell
them by their fruits.

Matthew 7:16–20

Centering prayer is a very pure prayer. It is a very simple
prayer. But not an easy one, precisely because it is so pure
and simple.

We poor humans like things that are complicated, that
are obviously hard. Then, when we have mastered them,
we can pat ourselves on the back for doing such a good
job. The false self is built up. We have accomplished
something. We have gotten something done.

But how can we pat ourselves on the back for having
accomplished something when all we have done is sit

there, using our prayer word, waiting upon an invisible God. It would seem any boob could do as much. There is certainly no sign that we are accomplishing anything.

That is the hard part of centering prayer. We humans are so production-oriented. We like to see the results of our labors. We want to see our time pay off. But at the end of twenty minutes of centering, what do we have to show for our time? It would seem absolutely nothing! All we can remember is precisely the times when we were not praying, when we were chasing after some thought or fantasy or tuning in on a passing noise. Or asking ourselves precisely what the use of all this is. Aren't we just wasting our time? Is anything going on? Or are we just falling asleep?

The fact is, the moments when we are in the prayer, we are in a realm of consciousness that is beyond that which the human memory can record. It is beyond reason. As Saint Paul puts it, "Eye has not seen, ear has not heard, not has it even entered into the human mind, what God has prepared for those who love him."

Well then, are we to just go ahead in purest faith without ever knowing if we are "doing it right," if this is really what God wants us to do—wasting twenty minutes twice a day just sitting here waiting for him to show up?

We are to go ahead in purest faith. There is no doubt about it. There is no other way we can practice the centering prayer: we sit there in faith and love. And we have to forget all about this stuff of "doing it right." That is the stuff of which the false self is created. We are not sitting there to do it right. We are sitting there to give ourselves in purest faith.

Yes, centering prayer is a very pure prayer. It is pure gift. We just simply give ourselves in faith and love to the

God of love, seeking nothing for ourselves. A song is not a song until it is sung, a bell is not a bell until it is rung, and love is not love until it is given away. Centering prayer is a giveaway; it is love.

But there is a way we can tell that this is what God really wants us to do. As Saint Paul says, "One sows, another reaps, but God gives the increase." Fruit comes from God—not from us. And "a sound tree produces good fruit." Centering prayer, by the activity of the Spirit of God flowing through us, does produce fruit in our lives.

For our part, our centering may seem to us to be a stark, barren winter tree, stripped naked, dead or dormant branches outlined by a dull grey winter sky. And so it might be at first. God works with us by following natural rhythms. Looking out my window now at the wintry scene, I see the dark woods at the end of the snow-covered lawn. It is March, and I know there is a lot of pulsating life out there. The sap is beginning to carry vital energies up from the roots. In a few weeks those seemingly dead trees will burst forth with life, immense profusions of colorful blossoms giving clear promise of autumn fruit. When we first sit in centering prayer, the Lord's work may indeed be hidden, but it is going on.

When I was a little kid, waiting for the sap to rise so we could put out our buckets for syrup, I could never wait till my knowing grandfather would say, "It is time." I would have to run out each day with my knife and gash a tree or two to see if anything was going on. The Lord has mercy on little ones. He does not want to see us gashing ourselves, looking for signs of life. So sometimes, according to our need, he gives us some sensible consolations, some peace, some overflowing light when we first begin to center.

This is great. If it happens, let us be grateful for it. But we need to beware of the danger. We cannot judge our centering by this. It is too ephemeral. And it would be false to judge a particular period of meditation "bad" because it did not leave us with these feelings of peace. God's real vitalizing action takes place at a much deeper level. It is creating abiding sources of lasting and constant peace, or rather, it is opening the channels so that the abiding Source of peace, the Holy Spirit, can freely act in our lives, producing the peace that only she can give. "A peace that the world cannot give, that is my gift to you."

Sometimes the fruits of centering prayer emerge quite quickly indeed. And it is usually others who notice them in our lives before we do. The Spirit's work is so subtle, she hides it from us. (She has to hide it from us, lest we begin to pat ourselves on the back for achieving it and, in the process, mess it all up.) There is a story I like to tell in connection with this.

I was sharing the centering prayer with a group of retreatants in the guesthouse at Saint Joseph's Abbey in Spencer, Massachusetts. As always, at the end of the retreat I was urging the men to be very good to themselves and make a real commitment to practice the prayer faithfully twice a day for sixty days, to give themselves a chance to see what God wanted to do in their lives. It was clear that they were there because God had brought them there. We don't do good things on our own. And he had brought them there precisely to learn this form of prayer. So it was clear that he wanted to do something with it in their lives.

He was inviting them to a new, deeper, and richer relationship with him.

Well, as I urged the men to make this commitment, one of them piped up. His name was Joe. "Father, are you kidding? With my six-ring circus! I got six kids running around at home. How am I going to find twenty minutes twice a day to sit quietly?" With my accustomed gentleness and compassion—they call it tough love!—I replied, "Joe, where there is a will, there is a way. You find time to eat. You find time to sleep. It is much more important to nurture and rest your spirit. Find the time. *Make it!*"

About six months later Joe returned to the Abbey for a retreat. I was not slow in approaching him. "Well, Joe, did you?"

"Yes, yes, Father, I did!" he replied. He went on, "I began to go into the office twenty minutes early in the morning and got my first meditation sitting at my desk, before my secretary came in. In the evening, when I come home from work, I always go in to wash up. Well, after I washed up, I began to sit in the tub for twenty minutes and got my second meditation there. Nobody noticed I was taking a little longer. Everything was going fine. Then one evening, after I had been meditating about three weeks, when I came out of the bathroom, there was my wife waiting for me. 'Joe, what's going on downtown? You come home these evenings, you are so happy and lively. You are bustling around with me and the kids. What's going on down at work? Why the big difference?' Oh boy! I knew I had to own up quick. So I told her what I had been doing. And you know what she said to me? 'Well, if you can meditate for twenty minutes before supper, I can meditate for twenty minutes before supper. When you come out of there, you can finish supper while I go in to meditate.' So now I have to finish fixing supper every night." Then he added, "But it's worth it. Has our home life and love life changed!"

For me, the point of the story is this: Joe at first hadn't noticed any difference at all. But in as little as three weeks his wife did see a big difference in him. He was leaving all the tensions of the day in the tub where he meditated and was able to be fully with his wife and children, enjoying his evenings with them. The Spirit was finding the freedom to produce in Joe's life her fruits of love, joy, peace, patience, and all those other fruits enumerated in Galatians 5.

We sit there in our meditation. And as far as we can tell during the time of the centering, or later when we look back at that time, nothing is going on. We are just sitting there, waiting on the Lord. But after we have been faithfully centering for a while, we need to look around at the rest of our life. And if we can't readily see anything different, let us ask that person who is walking closely with us on the journey if he or she sees any difference.

Last weekend we had a little centering prayer workshop here at Assumption Abbey. As is my usual practice, at the first session I invited the participants to tell us who they were, where they came from, and why they had come. The middle-aged woman (I hope she doesn't mind my so identifying her) at my right spoke up. After introducing herself, she added, "I've come because my husband came here for a workshop last August. It completely changed his life! I want the same." I didn't ask for details. It wasn't necessary. They were writ large on her face. Nor did I tell her that that glow betrayed the fact that, having learned the prayer from her husband and joined him in doing it each day, she had already found what she was looking for.

"I repeat, you will be able to tell them by their fruits."

Chapter 12

Lord, Lord

It is not anyone who says to me, "Lord, Lord," who will enter the kingdom of Heaven, but the person who does the will of my Father in heaven. When the day comes many will say to me, "Lord, Lord, did we not prophesy in your name, drive out demons in your name, work many miracles in your name?" Then I shall tell them to their faces: I have never known you; *away from me you evil doers!*

Matthew 7:21–23

"The kingdom of Heaven is within." And, indeed that is what we seek in centering prayer.

We certainly do not seek our own center or seek ourselves in any way. That is one of the reasons why centering prayer is totally different from self-hypnosis (in spite of what some who really do not understand the prayer say). We do not seek ourselves in any way. Nor do we seek anything for ourselves—peace or consolation or light.

We quite simply seek to enter into the kingdom of heaven, where God is all. We seek to enter into that state

where we can say in truth, "My God and my all." We seek
to be pure gift.

It is true that in centering prayer we do use a word, a
sacred word, a love word, or a prayer word, if you will.

Some have called it a mantra. Father John Main, who
has drawn together this ancient Christian method of
prayer taught by Saint John Cassian and a method of meditation he learned from a Hindu swami in Burma, does
teach the use of a mantra. But Father John's method is not
centering prayer as we have learned it from our Christian
tradition and teach it.

I am frankly quite unhappy when people speak of the
prayer word as a mantra—for one reason, because I think
we should have a great reverence for other religious traditions. I don't think we should take over their consecrated
terms and give them our own meanings. "Mantra" actually has several diverse meanings in the different schools
of Hindu philosophy. I respect those meanings. None of
them is the same as the meaning our tradition gives to the
prayer word.

Calling the prayer word a mantra can, and does, give
people the wrong impression. In this ancient Christian
method, the word is precisely a prayer word, a love word.
Prayer is a personal communication between a human
being and our true God, a loving communication. The
purpose of the word in centering prayer is wholly to foster
such a communication at a profoundly deep level, at the
level of being. Therefore we can readily call the word a
prayer word or a love word. The author of the little medi-
eval treatise *The Cloud of Unknowing,* a wise and holy old
monk, in instructing his spiritual son in regard to the
practice of the prayer, tells him, "Choose a word, a simple

word. A single-syllable word is best . . . But choose a word that is meaningful to you." And the meaning of the word is precisely this: giving ourselves to God in love.

It is true that the meaningful word we could choose for our centering prayer could be "Lord." And, thus, we could find ourselves in the course of the prayer saying "Lord, Lord." But our Lord here is not proclaiming the futility of our praying "Lord, Lord." What he is getting at here is praying without meaning our prayer, using a method or formula of prayer without truly praying.

Centering prayer got its popular name from the influence of that great spiritual master of our century Thomas Merton. One of the last words of life from this master, spoken to a group of friends in California just before he flew off to the East was this: "It's a risky thing to pray, and the danger is that our very prayers get between God and us. The great thing in prayer is not to pray, but to go directly to God. If saying your prayers is an obstacle to prayer, cut it out." What Merton is getting at here is the same thing as our Lord is saying.

If someone is indeed our lord, if we truly see him that way, then we seek to do exactly what he wants. He is the lord, we are the servants. His will is master. To say to God, "Lord, Lord," and then not to do what he wants, is to say words we do not mean. Rather than prayer, a true communication with God, our words are a lie. And no one who does not abide in the truth can enter into the kingdom of heaven.

Even if we choose another word, what our Lord says here holds true. Our prayer word, whatever word it might be—a name of the Lord, such as Jesus, God, Father, or Abba, or some other meaningful expression, such as "love," "friend," or "mine"—is essentially a love word. Its meaning is being to God in love. More than its meaning, its significance in the centering prayer is not what it in itself might mean but that of being a pointer, directing us wholly to the God who dwells within at the center of our being. And that direction is love. We are to God in faith and love. The word is but a reiteration of all that the prayer is. And it is of the very nature of love that we seek to please the one we love. We seek a union of mind and heart. We seek always to do the things that please. As Jesus declared, "I always do the things that please the Father."

To sit in centering prayer using any word whatsoever while we consciously refuse to do the will of God just doesn't work. We cannot enter into the kingdom of heaven while we are at odds with God—precisely because the Father, God, is in this heaven. The only way we can be with him in this state that is called heaven is in love. We cannot be with God, Father, in heaven and not know him, know him in the way that makes it impossible not to love him.

It all goes together really to say "Lord" or any other love word in truth, to be in heaven where the Father is, to love him, to be committed to doing his will—it is all the same thing. And to be known by the Son in the way he means it here, to be known by him as friend, is to be known in the way lovers know each other. To be known in the embrace of love. That is the only kind of knowing there can be in heaven. That is the only way we can be when we are in heaven. That is heaven.

We can prophesy without being one with the Lord like this. Prophecy is one of the charismatic gifts, given to the individual for the good of the community. It doesn't necessarily demand holiness on the part of the recipient. Moreover, there is false prophecy, when a prescient insight, whether natural or demonic, gives one a sense of the future or a natural or demonic force gives power to one's speech. We can drive out demons or work miracles in the name of the Lord without being united to him in spirit and heart. There is power in the name. It makes the evil ones tremble even when it is spoken out of the mouth of an evil one. It can work miracles to the glory of him whose name it is, even when it is spoken by an unworthy mouth.

Prophesying, casting out demons, and working miracles in the name of the Lord of themselves give us no claim upon the Lord. Only the love with which we do these things, and anything else, is what gives us a claim upon him. That of itself immediately brings us into his kingdom, into union with him, because *God is love.*

And this is the purity and power of centering prayer. Centering prayer is love. The prayer word is a love word, an expression of love, of giving ourselves to God in purest love. If the word we are using is not that, then we are not doing centering prayer. We may be doing a very relaxing exercise, finding some natural peace, sitting there repeating "Lord, Lord" or some other word, but we are not doing centering prayer if the word is not an expression of a love that compels us to seek to do always the things that please the Father.

True centering prayer cannot but bring us into the kingdom of heaven. We may not experience it in any sensible way. But in faith we know it is so. And we will see it in our lives as we become more and more determined to do the will of the Father in heaven.

Chapter 13

Follow Him—Wherever

When Jesus saw the crowd all about him he gave orders to leave for the other side. One of the scribes then came and said to him, "Master, I will follow you wherever you go." Jesus said, "Foxes have holes and the birds of the air have nests, but the Son of man has nowhere to lay his head."

Another man, one of the disciples, said to him, "Lord, let me go and bury my father first." But Jesus said, "Follow me, and leave the dead to bury their dead."

Matthew 8:18–22

"Master, I will follow you wherever you go." This is the basic attitude for centering prayer. We are willing to let go of everything and simply be to Jesus, with Jesus, wherever he leads. This is very simple and very pure love. We accept Jesus as our master, we have full confidence in him. During the time of the prayer we let go of all our own considerations, put both eyes on him and let him do with us as he will.

This attitude quickly enough spills over into the rest of our life. With it comes a great freedom, a complete trust, a sureness and joy about the way our life is unfolding. But it comes at a cost. Following Jesus into the center, following Jesus in his going to the Father in the Holy Spirit, does mean our leaving the familiar comfort of our own very human thoughts and images, our warm and fuzzy feelings.

The foxes have their holes and the birds of the air their nests. The animal part of us does have its feelings. And we do like to settle down in the warm comfort they can provide. We like feelings of peace and security and love and any other consolation the Lord might be willing to send along. And even if our thoughts and imagination do seem to fly all over the place even more when we sit down to meditate, we are happy if they will sometime settle down and nestle in.

But none of that belongs to centering prayer as such.

Certainly God can give us all sorts of consolations if he wills. And sometimes he does, especially during the first days, in order to encourage us in our weakness. But we have to learn just to let them be. If we start taking note of them or, worse, try to cultivate them, we are very much back in the false self, collecting things to build ourselves up.

During centering prayer on some days, there will be consolations that will make us feel very much at home during the prayer—the fox in his hole. But most days, that will probably not be the case. There will be little to satisfy the feelings and emotions. We might want to speak of dryness. I am not sure exactly what that means—maybe that we like wet, gooey feelings, feelings with lots of juice around them. In any case, in centering prayer, whether the feelings are flowing or completely dried up, it makes no difference. Our whole attention is to the Lord. Whenever we become aware of either—wetness or dryness—we follow the same "rule": we gently, lovingly return to the Lord with the use of our prayer word.

Thoughts and images will certainly keep whirring through our minds and imaginations. They never stop. We will probably become even more aware of them when we begin to meditate. Somehow most people, when they first begin to meditate, seem to think that they have to quiet the mind. Some forms of meditation do call for this. But not centering prayer. As the author of *The Cloud of Unknowing* tells his disciple:

> Be careful in this work and never strain your mind or imagination, for truly you will not succeed in this way. Leave these faculties at peace . . . Should some thought go on annoying you, demanding to know what you are doing, answer with this one word alone [your prayer word]. If your mind begins to intellectualize over the meaning and connotations of this little word, remind yourself that its value lies in its simplicity. Do this and I assure you these thoughts will vanish.

During centering prayer we just let the mind and imagination do what it will. Our prayer is at a deeper level. And anytime a thought or an image does captivate us, as soon as we become aware of it (and sometimes, when we do become aware, it seems to us that the thoughts have had us for quite a while), we gently return to the Lord at the center with the use of our prayer word.

Sometimes we think we would like to just settle down, turn off the thoughts and images, the feelings and emotions, and find some hole or nest where we could simply be. But that is not the lot of the follower of Christ. "The Son of man has nowhere to lay his head." We belong to the pilgrim people of God. We are ever on the journey. There is always room for more growth. The Lord wants to lead us ever more deeply into himself, into the mysteries of his love, and all of this is beyond our thoughts and images, our feelings and emotions, beyond the animal part and even beyond the human part. He would lead us, through the activity of the Holy Spirit, into the realms of his own divinity.

The surprising thing, though, is that through this, we do find a deep and very real rest and refreshment. "Come to me all you who labor and are heavily burdened, and you will find rest for your souls." The Lord does have a very compassionate concern and care for us, even though he seems a very exacting master.

This latter seems even more true in the next words the Lord addresses to one of his eager disciples: "Leave the dead to bury their dead." How harsh this sounds.

The prescription for centering prayer also sounds very harsh: whenever you become aware of *anything,* then simply, gently return to the Lord with the use of your prayer word. No exceptions. *Anything!* Good thoughts or bad thoughts, compassionate thoughts or caring thoughts. Everything is let go. Or to put it more accurately, we turn to the Lord and, in so doing, we leave these behind. It is complete discipleship.

And we do this with the consciousness that the thoughts and images we leave behind are dead. They are at least once, if not twice, removed from the living Reality. And we want the living Reality, the context within which all is alive, the Source of all life. In him we find all and we find it fully alive. "Through him all things came into being, not one thing came into being except through him. What has come into being in him is life." When, through the transformation of consciousness that centering prayer brings about, through the activity of the Holy Spirit in her gifts, God has indeed become the context of our thinking, then all our thoughts and images will be alive and life-giving.

But at first we must abandon them to let them take care of themselves. And, surprisingly enough, they do. We often have the experience that while we are centering and letting our thoughts run their own course, problems do clarify, ideas come together and develop, sermons and books are composed. This is one of the fringe benefits of centering prayer to which many a priest or writer like myself can attest.

At another level, we are again confronted with the heartlessness of centering prayer, especially those in ministry. There are so many in desperate need of our help. Not only the dead and those who surround them in grief but so many of the living, sometimes the living dead or the living who feel like they are dying or want to die. There is so much that needs to be done. How can we close our door and sit blissfully in prayer for twenty minutes while they wait outside?

I would say a few things in response to this. Even if we never closed our door, we could never respond to all the needs that are there for us. "The poor you will always have with you." If we don't close our door and take time to rest in the Source, we will in fact soon burn out, and then there will be no one there to heal any of the needy at our door.

Do we think we are more capable than our Lord himself? How many times in the course of his few years of ministry did he not send the crowd away and flee away to a solitary place, even when everyone was seeking, seeking him with their very legitimate and pressing needs. Even the Son of man needed his time with the Father to be refreshed and renewed for his ministry.

We should do all that God wants us to do. But we should not do more than God wants us to do. I suspect most dedicated people are going to have to answer to the Lord on Judgment Day for having done too much, for having tried to do what God himself wanted to do or wanted someone else to do. One of the surprises of centering prayer is that we discover that God can manage the world for twenty minutes without us—and not mess it up too much!

There is a time to follow the Master, follow him wherever—follow him into the realms beyond thought and image, feelings and emotions, follow him into the very center of God.

Chapter 14

In the Boat
of Centering Prayer

Then Jesus got into the boat followed by his disciples. Suddenly a storm broke over the lake, so violent that the boat was being swamped by the waves. But he was asleep. So they went to him and woke him saying, "Save us, Lord, we are lost!" And he said to them, "Why are you so frightened, you who have so little faith?" And then he stood up and rebuked the winds and the sea; and there was a great calm. They were astounded and said, "Whatever kind of man is this, that even the winds and the sea obey him?"

Matthew 8:23–27

We climb into the boat of centering prayer because we are following Jesus. It is because we believe in him, trust him, and love him that we do enter into the meditation. By faith we know this is where he is to be found, at the center of our being. And in our love we do want to be with him.

As we enter into centering prayer, we do feel like we are

leaving the firm ground of our clear rational thoughts and our even more solid images and feelings. We oftentimes do not realize how ephemeral these really are. They are ours. We seem to have some control over them. And so we think they are something solid we can count on.

But when we begin to center, we soon enough discover how little control we do have over them. Whether we like it or not, they keep surging around in our heads and even in our bodies. Thoughts of all sorts come up and go in all directions. Images too—the strangest things. Here we are about a most holy task, and even the most unseemly and ungodly sort of things appear. And our feelings. They are not always what we would like them to be. We are very much at sea.

We would, indeed, like everything to calm down. "A little quiet please while I meditate and rest with the Lord." But instead, just the opposite seems to occur. When we quiet down for the prayer, we suddenly discover how much has been going on inside of us while we have been busy outside. No wonder we are so exhausted at the end of a day.

We get tossed about by all these thoughts and feelings. They seem to prevent us from doing what we want to do, from heading in the direction we want to go. Progress in centering prayer—whatever that might be—seems to completely elude us. Day after day we sit there and the thoughts rage on, tossing us this way and that. Things don't seem to be getting any better. It is tough to keep going. Our practice is in danger of foundering.

And where is Jesus in the midst of all of this? We undertook this practice of centering prayer in order to be with him, closer to him, going his way. And where is he?

He might have seemed very present at first, everything going smoothly, lots of peace. We did seem to be making some real progress. But if that was ever the case for us, it didn't last very long. The Lord sometimes gives us some real consolations when we first begin centering prayer. We can almost feel his presence or even actually feel it. He seems actually to speak to us. At least, he is very present, with all his love and care. It can be quite wonderful. He knows his beginners often need encouragement, need to know he is with them in the boat or they will never shove out from shore. But once he gets us going, he knows what we really need, and he seems to disappear. We wish we could at least say for certain that he is asleep. Rather, he seems to be wholly absent.

"Save us, Lord." Our prayer word sometimes seems to become just such a cry for help. A cry in the dark, in the midst of a storm. The thoughts and feelings seem to overwhelm us. We can't escape them. They push us around. Sometimes very black and threatening thoughts and feelings arise. People have been known to burst into tears when they first begin to center, so great is the fear. If we have been very solidly tied to our false self, we can indeed feel as if we are perishing as it begins to float away from us. We do not yet know the deep serenity and security of the true self. What have we? We perish and the Lord seems to take no care.

Where are you, Lord? Is this what I came to centering prayer for?

Yes.

I am afraid the Lord can say to most of us, "You have so little faith." Why are we so frightened?

We are frightened because we really don't trust the

Lord. Oh, we have some faith. Otherwise we would not be centering. The prayer begins with faith and love.

We are like that royal official who came up from Capernaum to Cana to ask Jesus to restore his sick son to health. The good man would not have left the bedside of his dying child and made the difficult journey up into the hill country if he had not had some very real faith. And we would not sit in our chair when we could be using those twenty minutes for so many other good and productive things, if we did not have some very real faith. Nonetheless, Jesus chided the man: "Unless you people see signs and wonders, you do not believe." We tend to doubt the validity or efficacy of our prayer if we don't have "lights," good thoughts or at least good warm feelings, sensible consolations of one sort or another so we can know we are being heard and what we are doing is pleasing to the Lord.

"Return home," Jesus told him. "Your son will live." "Return to the center" (our true home, the home where the Father and the Son and the Holy Spirit dwell to make their home with us), the Lord tells us. "You won't die; only the false self will die. You will be made whole, you will find all you want, you will arrive where you want to be."

Saint John tells us that when the man was on his way home, his servants met him with the news that his son was going to live. We can imagine with how much more joy he continued on his journey after receiving the news. But if his faith had been all that it could have been, he would have had as much joy in his sure knowledge from Jesus' word as he received from the report of his servants.

If we do not find as much joy as we would like in our

centering prayer, what is the cause? It is our lack of faith. What can we do about it? A number of things.

First and most important, we can be faithful to our practice. We can continue to return home. And in time, we will see in our lives the tangible proof of the working of the Lord, the growth and ripening of the fruits of the Spirit. And probably even before we see it ourselves, others, like the servants of the father, will come to tell us about it.

We can reach out and get partners in centering. We can invite our loved ones, our family, to do it with us. We can form a group. We can teach it to those to whom we minister and do it with them. In doing it with others, we will experience the witness of their faith and it will strengthen our faith.

We can share with others who are centering. Let them tell us of the fruits in their lives. This will encourage our faith and help us to see the fruits in our own life.

Finally, we can do some reading and let the authors, or rather the Holy Spirit through the authors, speak to us the word of faith, the faith-building word. Let us give some time each day to the Sacred Scriptures, letting the Lord himself speak to us through his inspired and inspiring Word. We can read about centering prayer itself. (There is a bibliography at the end of this volume which might assist in finding helpful books.) And we can read other, more general books that will nurture our faith.

In time, we come to know that the Lord is indeed with us whenever we center. In time, there comes an increasing calm, not only during centering but throughout our whole life. But by then, we are not so concerned about the calm. We are rather filled with a growing sense of this God who does dwell at our center, always with us as we sail through life. We have a mounting confidence. Our fears die away even as the raging of the thoughts and images dies away. We begin to be filled with the question, "Whatever kind of man is this?" We long to know and understand him more and more. With eagerness we climb into his boat of centering, to have some time with him away from all the crowd of the day. We no longer feel "at sea," feel that the many thoughts and images are a storm impeding our progress. We are very content just to be with him, living in the awesome excitement of a question, of a relationship that each day opens out to even greater wonder.

Something deep within us says, in that silence that is beyond all words, "It is wonderful to be with Jesus in the boat of centering prayer."

Chapter 15

❖

A New Wineskin for Fasters

Then John's disciples came to him and said, "Why is it that we and the Pharisees fast, but your disciples do not?" Jesus replied, "Surely the bridegroom's attendants cannot mourn as long as the bridegroom is still with them? But the time will come when the bridegroom is taken away from them, and then they will fast. No one puts a piece of unshrunken cloth onto an old cloak, because the patch pulls away from the cloak and the tear gets worse. Nor do people put new wine into old wineskins; otherwise, the skins burst, the wine runs out, and the skins are lost. No; they put new wine in fresh skins and both are preserved."

Matthew 9:14–17

Our Master and Teacher seems to go a bit overboard here with his use of metaphors: bridegroom and fasting, old cloth and new, wineskins and new wine—all in a few sentences, one paragraph. Our Lord has so much he wants to say to us and so little time to say it. He is eager to leave words behind and enter into a communion of being with us where he can give us his all, that all that is much too much for human words, no matter how many metaphors he might use.

There are times on our spiritual journey when the Lord, the Bridegroom, is indeed with us. These periods of presence, consolation, and joy are to be relished. They usually don't last a lifetime. At such times, when he is so present, we hardly need a method of prayer or any of the ordinary supports. We just simply pray, as he leads us, usually in good part according to the particular temperament he has given us. Words, feelings, images may abound or we may be drawn deep, deep into the silence within, where God speaks by silence, where the eternal Word and he alone, the Bridegroom, is heard. When the Bridegroom is so present, it is no time for mourning or fasting or anything else on our part but only for being a wide-open yes.

"But the time will come when the bridegroom is taken away." And then it will be a time of fasting, whether we like it or not. There are no rich consolations, no "lights," no feelings or emotions to sustain and nourish us in our prayer. It becomes a time of dark faith. It is now that we need the support and guidance of an authentic method of prayer, for there is the danger that we will not accept the fast, that we will not be content to meet the Lord and wait upon him in the darkness of faith. We are tempted to begin to try to create our own light, engender feelings and emotions—in short, make prayer our project rather than a response to the Divine, following his leadings.

It is at a time like this that an ancient and revered Christian method of prayer such as centering prayer can be invaluable to us. But we must take care not to put a piece of unshrunken cloth onto an old cloak. We do not want to try to understand or practice centering prayer in the light of what we have known or experienced in conceptual or affective prayer.

Unless we are led into an extraordinary period of very intense purification, there usually will be a time in a daily program when we will be listening to the Lord, especially in Scriptures, and respond to him with words and thoughts and affections. No one fasts all the time. But we will want something more. These thoughts and images and feelings are shrunken cloth. Directly or indirectly they have been drawn from the experience of God. But they are not the experience itself. They are one or two or more steps removed from that experience. They are human creations that can do little more than point toward the Divine, but in no adequate way express him.

We want the experience of God himself. We need unshrunken cloth, a mind and a heart that is wide open, with no limits, so that God himself can walk in. It is time to let go of the old cloak, for our thoughts and images at best do cloak reality. When we make love, we do not want any clothes in the way, no matter how beautiful they might be or how much they might tell us about the person who wears them. We want to be completely free to be to the person.

Our thoughts and images are like the images we see in the stained glass windows in our churches or in the great cathedral of Chartres. They are magnificent, full of color and life. And they are there to tell us something about God and his wondrous doings of love. But in so doing, they allow in little of the light. A clear glass allows in the full light of the sun. Centering prayer allows in the full light of the Son.

When the Bridegroom comes to ravish our spirit, he needs no clothes. We do not want any thoughts or images to hold him back from us, we want only him.

In the normal course of things there comes a time when affective prayer and discursive meditation seem to "dry up." Or, at least, the old cloak no longer meets all our needs. If we sense that our old way of praying is no longer really giving us what we want and if we thus decide to begin to seek contemplative union with God through centering prayer, we must take care not to sew this unshrunken cloth on the old. If we come to centering prayer with the same expectations with which we came to discursive meditation, we will indeed be even more torn by frustration. The fact is, we must come to centering prayer with no expectations.

God's gracious call to contemplation, which is what we are experiencing when we experience a yearning for more, is new wine. It cannot be kept in the old skins of discursive meditation. They cannot hold it. If we try, our prayer will be experienced as dry and unsatisfying. Chances are that it will fall apart and we will give up. Our prayer life may perish completely. When God calls us to contemplation, to a more simple, quiet, deep union with him, we have to move on. The wine of grace that was in the old skins has run out. God-given lights and consolations, strength for the journey, will no longer be found in the old methods of prayer. We have to put the new wine of his contemplative call into new wineskins.

Centering prayer is a new wineskin. Age-old though this method be, it is ever fresh and flexible. In its simplic-

ity it has all the space we will ever need, no matter how
exuberant and heady the divine fermentaion might become. We sit there, wide open, and let the Lord do whatever he wants. Yet the little structure it does provide is
extremely important. By providing space regularly in our
busy lives for contemplation, it keeps the graces of contemplation from being lost or dissipated. Preserving them,
it allows them to mature until we come to know that this
is the wine which delights the human heart.

Chapter 16

❖

In Their Love

At that time Jesus exclaimed, "I bless you, Father,
Lord of heaven and of earth, for hiding these things
from the learned and the clever and revealing them to
little children. Yes, Father, for that is what it pleased
you to do. Everything has been entrusted to me by
my Father, and no one knows the Son except the
Father, just as no one knows the Father except the
Son and those to whom the Son chooses to reveal
him."

Matthew 11:25–27

Certainly a wonderful model for centering prayer is the
little child in his father's arms. A true father is always
delighted to have his little one in his arms. He doesn't
much care if the child is squirming about a bit, looking
this way and that or pulling his beard or just resting there
or sleeping peacefully. As long as his child is there in his
arms, the father is content.

In centering prayer we, as it were, settle in our Father's
arms, or more truly, in his heart. Our thoughts may go this

way and that. Different things outside us may catch our attention for the moment. We might even doze off. But as long as we stay there, each time we catch ourselves straying, returning with our love word, our Father is very pleased.

A little child knows his father's love. He does not have to struggle with any of the rationalizations of the teenager. He doesn't feel the adolescent's need to separate himself, in order to find himself. Indeed, if one learns centering prayer at an early age and comes to know and experience his true self in God, he or she will escape many of the traumas of adolescence and not feel the need to alienate himself from parents and Mother Church.

Our heavenly Father is an all-good and provident father. Mysteriously, though, his providential love and care is exercised and manifested in this world in and through our prudence. Once we are able to exercise prudence he entrusts everything to us. He has made us in his own image. He gives us our freedom. He gives us the guidance of the natural law, of his revelation, and of his Church. His grace is sufficient for us. With these, the rest is up to us.

It is true, only the Father knows the Son. We will know Jesus only when the Father has revealed to us his own divinity. Only then can we know who Jesus really is, as he is, one with the Father in that divinity. This revelation is beyond anything our rational minds can grasp, beyond all our thoughts and images. It is only when we are willing to leave our very limited and limiting concepts behind and enter into the cloud of unknowing that we will hear the Father say, "This is my beloved Son," that we will know Jesus as the only Son of the Father.

And it is only Jesus, the only-begotten Son, who can

reveal the Father to us. For he alone truly knows the Father. Through the revelation, he leads us to the Father, through the Gospels and through the action of the Holy Spirit. Where the mind leaves off, the heart goes on, we are told by that great theologian Saint Thomas Aquinas. Love-knowledge, that spiritual instinct that is brought about in us by the action of the Holy Spirit in the gifts, brings us into the very heart of the Trinity. We come to "know" what it means that we have been baptized into Christ, made one with him. In some very real way, beyond anything we can adequately think or express, we have been made one with Christ the Son. We are one with the Son to the Father in the Holy Spirit. In this way the Son reveals the Father to us.

We are brought within and rest in the very embrace of God. Centering prayer allows us in some way to experience this, as it opens us to the action of the Holy Spirit in us through the gifts of wisdom, understanding, and knowledge. Resting in this embrace we find wonderful peace, deep joy, a peace this world cannot give, Christ's own peace.

When I was a little boy, I used to spend my summers on my grandparents farm in Kansas, just outside of Wichita. In the evenings, when the day's doings were done and the stillness of night was coming upon us, I used to sit on the top step of the front porch. I could sit there for hours in the deepest contentment. Granddad would come out and take his place at one end of the porch swing. Perhaps he would have the evening paper with him. After the dishes were done, Grandma would join us. And she might bring along some knitting or the like. But as the light faded, the paper and the knitting would be set aside, and we would all just sit there in the silence, listening to the growing sounds of night. This is perhaps one of the happiest memories of my childhood. And now I realize why I was so filled with contentment and joy as I sat there whiling away the evening hours.

My grandparents had been married over seventy-five years when the Lord finally called them home. They loved each other deeply. As they sat there in the evening, in the silence, a wonderful communion of love flowed between them. And I was caught up into that wonderful love. I knew a security that was complete.

Psychologists tell us that the most important thing for a little child is not his mother's love, although we might well have thought that to be the case. Nor the father's. Rather, the most important thing for the child is the love the mother and father have for each other. Herein the little one finds true security, the space to grow, the bonding that will eventually enable him or her to let go and stand secure in his own being.

The sad reality is that this is something very rare in our society today. All too often there is no father. A single or divorced mother copes with the child alone. And even when the parents are both present, oftentimes it is not a togetherness of mind and heart, a bonding in nurturing love.

This is one of the areas in which centering prayer can be tremendously healing. Someone who has never known the secure space of parents' mutual love or has known it for too short a time can learn to sit in the security of the love of the Father and the Son in the Holy Spirit. Even those of us who have been fortunate enough to have had parents who deeply loved each other and nurtured us in that loving space can yet grow more in the experience of this. For our parents, however good as they may have been and however rich in their love, were, like ourselves, poor sinful creatures and, in their sinfulness, failed us to some extent. We have all been wounded by our parents' limitations and failures. Part of growing up is to accept this, wholeheartedly forgive our parents, and do what we can to help them to grow into completeness and freedom. But even when we do forgive them fully, the wounds remain. The damage is done. We ourselves need healing, a healing that in part our parents can give us as they continue to grow. But we can find the fullness of healing, and sometimes very quickly, by allowing ourselves to rest in the divine embrace in centering prayer.

Our Lord has said, "Unless you become as a little one, you cannot enter into the kingdom of Heaven." This is very true of centering prayer. We must needs become very little, leaving off all our doings, and let the Father and his beloved Son bring us into the kingdom of their love. Let Go, Let God, is a good motto here. If we do, we will enter into the kingdom, for the Father will reveal the Son to us, and the Son will reveal the Father, and this knowledge of the Father and the Son in the Holy Spirit is indeed the kingdom of heaven.

Chapter 17

❖

The Way to Unity and Peace

Knowing what was in their minds Jesus said to them, "Every kingdom divided against itself is heading for ruin; and no town, no household divided against itself can last. Now if Satan drives out Satan, he is divided against himself; so how can his kingdom last? And if it is through Beelzebul that I drive devils out, through whom do your own experts drive them out? They shall be your judges, then. But if it is through the Spirit of God that I drive out devils, then be sure that the kingdom of God has caught you unawares . . . Make a tree sound and its fruit will be sound; make a tree rotten and its fruit will be rotten. For the tree can be told by its fruit. You brood of vipers, how can your speech be good when you are evil? For words flow out of what fills the heart. Good people draw good things from their store of goodness; bad people draw bad things from their store of badness."

Matthew 12:25–28, 33–35

Most of the time we are each a kingdom that is divided. The kingdom of God is within and we are without. What is more, we are even divided in our outward activity.

How often when we are supposed to be praying, have even chosen to pray, do we not find that we are thinking of many other things. Our mind is here and there, remembering the past, projecting the future, regretting what was, fearing what will be. And our heart gets very much into it too, even though we might still be reciting prayers, singing hymns, letting the beads pass through our fingers.

And this does not only happen in our times of prayer. When we are with friends or colleagues, listening to a client or a student, watching a TV program, or so on, we often find we have been elsewhere and have accomplished little of what we had intended.

Often the division goes even further. While part of us is doing all this, another part of us is watching ourselves do it, evaluating, appraising, assessing. We have torn ourselves into a subject who is doing all of this and an object whom we ourselves are scrutinizing.

With all of this we are indeed headed for ruin. Burning the candle at both ends and at so many levels, we end up one big drip. This is called burnout. And if we don't burn out, the sheer multitude of things going on in us wears us out and we sooner or later give up.

Not being together ourselves, within ourselves, how can we possibly see ourselves as at one with others. The town, the household, the community, the Body of Christ is indeed divided. Instead of seeing the other members as one with us, celebrating their victories as our victories, working to build them up, supporting them in every way we can, we rather see them as competitors. We throw up our defenses. We do not invite them to help us, to support and encourage us; we don't even have a hope that that is possible. Competition is the name of the game.

We see the sad results in the Church. The community for whom Christ prayed "that they may be one" is divided into countless sects—and very sad to say, warring sects: in northern Ireland, in Lebanon, and even in the Holy Land in the holy places themselves, in the very sepulcher of the Lord. Christianity continues to divide and day by day becomes a smaller minority within the human family.

And we see it within that family too. The human family is a very divided family. Strife tears it apart. Among nations and within nations, competition has constantly led to armed strife, unbelievable destruction and widespread starvation. The possibility of total ruin is at hand as massive stockpiles of weaponry wait ready to deal the death blow to humanity and its environment.

What hope is there? How can this be turned around?

It must begin with the individual. When an individual comes together within himself, he or she comes to know oneness not only with God but with all the rest of the creation, every woman, man, and child, all sentient life, all that comes forth from the ever-creative hand of God. With that knowledge of oneness comes care, reverence, good stewardship, affirmation, and communion.

There is probably no more effective way that one can come to this oneness within than through contemplative prayer, centering prayer. With the help of a word of love we begin to put both eyes on God, our whole attention with all the affections of our heart. Opening ourselves thus to the divine, to the action of the Holy Spirit, we begin to see things as they really are, the oneness of all in God. We become effective agents for unity.

Disunity was sewn into us with original sin. It was fostered by the whole environment within which we grew up. Much healing is needed within ourselves as well as outside ourselves. But it must first be done within before we can hope to begin to effect it without. How often those who went to witness and work for peace, for the end of the hateful divisions of oppression and prejudice, have themselves fallen prey to violence, have given way to hatred and soon enough fallen away. We must first look to ourselves. We open to the needed healing, we find the unity that exists deep within us, when we sit in centering prayer. Gradually the divisions are healed. We are able to be all there, and where we are we find ourselves there. We know our oneness with all and so bring a compassionate healing love to all.

Some have expressed the fear that when we sit in the silence, letting go of all our thoughts, we open ourselves to Beelzebul, to the evil spirits. The Fathers and the great teachers of prayer through the centuries, clear on our Lord's teaching that the kingdom of God is within, have strongly asserted that it is impossible for the evil one to invade those deep recesses of the human person. The evil spirits can at most invade the body, as they do in the rather rare instances of diabolical possession. More frequently they influence the human spirit through the feelings and emotions, which have their seat in the body, though they touch immediately on the soul. In centering prayer we wisely disregard all feelings and emotions, and so give no place to the evil one to influence us. Rather, we go to that deeper place, the kingdom of God, and abide with him, not only safe and free from the evil one but nurtured, enlightened, and healed by the Lord himself.

The Lord gives us the clear sign by which we can know this is so: "The tree can be told by its fruit." As we practice centering prayer, peace, that harmony of order, will grow in us and then around us. We will know our oneness with others, with the Lord, with the whole creation. Good fruit like this does not come from Beelzebul. "Good people draw good things from their store of goodness."

It never ceases to amaze me that such a simple little thing like sitting quietly with the Lord for twenty minutes twice a day can have such momentous effects in our lives and make us agents of the good. I teach centering prayer with conviction and joy and make these claims for it, because I have seen what it has done in my own life and in the lives of others; great people, who have done great things, like Cardinal Bernardin and Mrs. Aquino. And hidden little people—who are perhaps doing even greater things—like some of the brothers in my own monastery and some of the lay persons whom I have the privilege to serve. I can only urge you to be truly faithful to your practice and you will not only see all the wounds in your own heart healed, but you will find an openness growing in you for God. And the God of surprises will do surprising things with you. And perhaps soon enough you will find yourself singing with Mary and so many of her children who have followed this way:

My soul magnifies the Lord
and my spirit rejoices in God, my savior.
For he has looked on the lowliness of his servant.
Yes, from henceforth all generations will call me blessed
for he that is mighty has done great things for me.
Holy is his name!

Chapter 18

❖

Mothering the Christ

Jesus was speaking to the crowds when suddenly his
mother and his brothers were standing outside and
were anxious to have a word with him. But to the
man who told him this Jesus replied, "Who is my
mother? Who are my brothers?" And stretching out
his hand towards his disciples he said, "Here is my
mother and my brothers. Anyone who does the will
of my Father in heaven is my brother and sister and
mother."

Matthew 12:46–50

Literally this text is about Mary and all those who, like
her, have learned to say a complete yes to God. Mary's yes
was so absolutely complete, she was so totally open to the
divine in body and soul, in her whole being, that God took
of her flesh and became one with us. Mary is the mother
of Jesus not only in the spirit but even in the flesh. She is
totally mother of God. Her whole being is about mothering, mothering the whole Christ, her divine Son and each
one of us who have become one with him through his

saving grace. She always seeks, and always did seek, to do the will of her Father in heaven.

But let us take a look at some of the spiritual meaning that can be found in this passage.

There are those who stay outside when they want to communicate with the Lord, to pray to him. They pray with words, thoughts, and ideas, rather than with their very being. They send these words to God, whom they sense as being at some distance, perhaps off in his heavens or in the tabernacle. Perhaps even within them, but not as one with them. They are sending word in. It is still subject to subject, not realizing their deep intersubjective union with God. Their thoughts, ideas, concepts, and images stand as a crowd around the Lord. They stand between the Lord and those who pray.

In centering prayer we bypass this crowd. We are like the infirm young man who was brought to Jesus on one occasion. Again there was a pressing crowd and there seemed no possibility of getting right to Jesus. But his devoted friends who had brought him there were not going to be put off. They scaled the roof, tore off some tiles, and lowered the young man on his pallet till he swung right there in front of Jesus. In centering prayer we go right to the center, where Jesus ever dwells as our most intimate lover. He is there for us. And the little method of centering prayer, like those devoted friends, helps us to bypass all the crowding thoughts and images and come to rest right there in the center with Jesus, to be healed by him and made whole.

It was the Lord himself who gently led me into centering. As my prayer simplified through my high school years, I would spend more time just looking at the taber-

nacle or at the Host exposed in the monstrance, something much more common back in those days. Gradually I
became more and more aware of his presence within me,
and my centering became more constant. When I entered
the monastery, the novice master—Lord rest his soul!—
presumed we raw recruits knew little or nothing about
prayer. He proceeded to teach us a method of discursive
meditation. Try as I might, I couldn't get very far with it
and found it very distracting. Certainly not refreshing. I
went to the father abbot, the saintly Dom Edmund, with
my difficulties. He asked me how I had been praying.
Then he assured me that the way the Lord had led me was
an authentic way to pray, and encouraged me to continue
in it, giving me more knowledge and understanding of this
traditional practice.

Father Edmund called the prayer "the prayer of the
will." In it, we unite our wills with God's will, or rather
with an act of the will, in love, we reach out to embrace
what is—our oneness with God in Christ. At baptism we
are brought into a oneness with Christ that is beyond
anything we can fully comprehend. It is an ontological
union, a union at the level of being and grace. To be true
to this then, to be true to who we are, we want to will
exactly the same as God Christ wills. The Lord wants an
intimate personal union with us as well as a union in
being. At the Last Supper he had prayed that we would be
one with him even as he is one with the Father. He and
the Father are absolutely one, yet as two distinct persons
they embrace each other in a love that so completely expresses who they are that that love is the divine; it is
another person who completely possesses, or rather is, the
divinity, the Holy Spirit. Saint Bernard, in his explanation

of those divine love poems that constitute the Song of Songs, tells us that the Holy Spirit is the Kiss of the Father and the Son, the communion of persons whereby they so completely breathe forth themselves to each other in love that that love is their very divinity.

We might well think of centering prayer as kissing God, kissing him with that divine Kiss who is the Holy Spirit. Saint Paul reminds us that "we cannot pray as we ought but the Holy Spirit prays within us." At baptism, when we were made partakers of the divine life and nature, the Holy Spirit was given to us as our spirit—the gift of God most high. He dwells in us ever ready to express our love for God in a love that will be totally worthy and adequate for God. He can do this, though, only when we are willing to let go of all our own expressions of love, our little thoughts and feelings and images, and are willing to just be, with the total openness of our being—that being which is made in the very image of God and has had his likeness restored to it in baptism. Then the Holy Spirit prays within us, being the divine Kiss whereby we kiss our God of love. Here the intercourse is complete. And it is fruitful, bringing forth, first within us but then to be brought forth and shared with the world, all the fruits of the Spirit.

Union with God is always an effective union. It *does the will of the Father in heaven.* If we are truly praying when we center, truly giving over our will to God, wanting only him, then the fruits of the Spirit will grow and ripen in our lives. As our Lord has repeatedly told us, we can judge the tree—our centering prayer practice—by its fruits. Not only will it produce joy and peace within and make us agents of joy and peace for those around us, but we will be persons of love, reaching to others with care and compassion, in ways that are compatible with our particular role in the Body of Christ. And perhaps love will even call us forth in some very surprising ways too.

I have already shared with you the story of Ferdinand Mahfood, the founder of Food for the Poor. Let me tell you the story of another man.

A man of exceptional charm and ability, Carl Shelton was very successfully climbing the corporate ladder. With his high level of dedication, he could well have reached the very top and situated his family in the lap of luxury. But Carl began to take his discipleship of Jesus Christ seriously; through centering prayer his life became centered. He soon left the corporate scene and established a small business in San Diego which would enable him to get his boys through college, prepare for the diaconate, and discern how best to use his uncanny business sense for the Lord. After a month with Mother Teresa in Calcutta, Carl decided to do something about feeding the hungry. But as a true leader, he had too much respect for his fellow human to aim at any sort of patronizing giveaway program. Every person has the right to help himself.

S.H.A.R.E. (Self-Help And Resource Exchange) was born and within a year it was sharing over a million pounds of food a month on this side of the border in San Diego and distributing larger and larger amounts among the poorest of the poor across the border in San Diego's impoverished sister city of Tijuana.

Shelton's idea was simple but ingenious. He would get large producers to sell him enormous quantities of foodstuffs at reduced prices (or even donate them). Those participating in the program—thousands of families now in cities across the United States—would pay twelve dollars and two hours of community service for sixty to seventy pounds of mixed foodstuffs, which would always include meat, bread, vegetables, and fruit. The two hours of service provide the labor force to handle the foodstuffs, preparing the seventy-pound packages and distributing them, to care for the office work, and to distribute the giveaway food to the totally impoverished.

Rather than creating a whole new organizational octopus, Shelton networks many existing ones which he calls "host organizations." These preexisting local groups enroll participants from among their membership, collect their monies, supervise their community service (up to 50 percent of which can be used by the local organization for its own ministries), and distribute the food packages. Others who do not need food assistance but want to be a part of S.H.A.R.E. can be sponsors, providing funds for those who cannot afford even the twelve-dollar fee and rendering services, like the many truckers who get the food to the distribution points. At the time of the monthly food distribution any one of these points—above all, the main warehouse—takes on an almost carnival atmosphere, a hardworking one, as people help people and everybody profits while community is built. There are no racial, color, creedal, or even poverty requirements to be a participant in S.H.A.R.E. Government handouts are not a part of S.H.A.R.E.'s self-help program, but it is the donated community services that do make it possible for S.H.A.R.E. to distribute large quantities of foodstuffs gratis to the completely deprived on both sides of the border. S.H.A.R.E. San Diego, which was the first and to a large extent the model for all the other local S.H.A.R.E.s, each of which has its own degree of autonomy, is backed by the diocese and unites more than two hundred other host organizations—schools, labor unions, housing associations, community groups, and churches of many traditions. It is truly ecumenical.

Most who begin to practice centering prayer will never have the creative ability or enormous daring that Deacon Shelton has to express their growing love and compassion in such striking fashion. But I can promise you that if you practice centering prayer faithfully and generously, you will find yourself doing things that you would never have imagined possible. Our God is a God of surprises, and he makes us surprised and surprising people.

However the Lord might lead us, we will, all of us, through our centering prayer, become a mother of Christ, first of all mothering the Christ within ourselves, collaborating with the Father as we are made into the image of his Firstborn. And then in others. (What is more motherly than feeding a hungry child?) We will be a compassionate sister or brother to Christ in each of our sisters and brothers. We will, with all our hearts and being, want to do "the will of our Father in heaven."

Chapter 19

❖

Enriching the Soil

Jesus said, "Listen, a sower went out to sow. As he sowed, some seeds fell on the edge of the path, and the birds came and ate them up. Others fell on patches of rock where they found little soil and sprang up at once, because there was no depth of earth, but as soon as the sun came up they were scorched and, not having any roots, they withered away. Others fell among thorns, and the thorns grew up and choked them. Others fell on rich soil and produced their crop, some a hundred fold, some sixty, some thirty. Anyone who has ears should listen!"

Then the disciples went up to him and asked, "Why do you talk to them in parables?" In answer, he said, "Because to you is granted to understand the mysteries of the kingdom of Heaven, but to them it is not granted. Anyone who has will be given more and will have more than enough; but anyone who has not will be deprived even of what he has. The reason I talk to them in parables is that they look without seeing and listen without hearing or understanding.

So in their case what was spoken by the prophet Isaiah is fulfilled:

> *Listen and listen, but never understand!*
> *Look and look, but never perceive!*
> *This people's heart has grown coarse,*
> *their ears dulled, they have shut their eyes tight*
> *to avoid using their eyes to see, their ears to hear,*
> *their heart to understand,*
> *changing their ways and being healed by me.*

"But blessed are your eyes because they see, your ears because they hear! In truth I tell you, many prophets and upright people longed to see what you see, and never saw it; to hear what you hear, and never heard it.

"So pay attention to the parable of the sower. When anyone hears the word of the kingdom without understanding, the Evil One comes and carries off what was sown in his heart: this is the seed sown on the edge of the path. The seed sown on patches of rock is someone who hears the word and welcomes it at once with joy. But such a person has no root deep down and does not last; should some trial come, or some persecution on account of the word and at once he falls away. The seed sown in thorns is someone who hears the word, but the worry of the world and the lure of riches choke the word and so it produces nothing. And the seed sown in rich soil is someone who hears the word and understands it; this is the one who yields a harvest and produces now a hundredfold, now sixty, now thirty."

Matthew 13:4–23

"Listen!" That is the key word here. Jesus, the Word, the only adequate expression of the Father, calls upon us to listen so that we may not only hear this Word but be formed and recreated by it, to his own likeness, we who are the image of the Father through creation.

Jesus calls us to listen and then he goes on to speak about listening. Each of us is a listening. Listening is not just something we do or have; we are a listening. Already, genetically, and even more radically through original sin, our listening has been shaped. It was further shaped by our environment, by all the behavioral influences that surrounded us in our most formative years. Prejudices were bred into us as surely and as deeply as any other habits and outlooks. So we come to this encounter with the Word of God as a certain listening.

Some of us can be likened to the hardened well-trodden path. All sorts of things can come our way and make no impression whatsoever, unless perhaps a good rain of grace should soften us up. Ah, yes! We hear the Word of God, perhaps in the liturgy, perhaps even in our own reading or in a Bible study group. The Word of God actually speaks to us all day long, through creation, through events (there is a loving Providence behind them all), through each one who walks into our lives. But, alas, it comes and it goes. How often have you had the experience I have had (I am embarrassed to say) of standing attentively (?) through the proclamation of the Gospel at the Eucharist and even listening to a homily on the Word but an hour later being unable even to say what Gospel was read that day?

There is ceaseless coming and going in our life and we never stop—really stop—to listen; we live on the path. We

hear and we hear, but we never hear. What Georgia
O'Keeffe said of seeing applies equally of listening; indeed
seeing is just listening with a different faculty:

> Still—in a way—nobody sees a flower—really—
> it is so small—we haven't time
> and to see takes time, like to have a friend takes time.

The Word speaks to us through all that is. Some of us
are a little better at listening, but we harbor prejudices that
are as hard as rock. What openness there is is all hedged
about by them. Any truth, because it is an expression of
him who is the Truth, has a way of seeping down and
expanding, demanding more and more of us. When the
heat's on, when our prejudices are threatened, especially
those prejudices that make up that false identity we harbor
as the self—the false self—we quickly enough let the word
wither. It finds no nurture in us.

As I have said before, that false self is made up of what
we do and what we have and what we think others think
of us. When we see ourselves this way, our doings and
havings are very important; they are all that we have (so
we think). So they tend to take up a lot of room in our
lives and choke out everything else. We may indeed be
trying to cultivate a "spiritual life," but our activities and
concerns leave little room for it.

Centering prayer creates in us good, rich soil. In the
moments of centering we are wide open to receive all that
the Word has to give us. We let go of everything else; we
are a boundless listening for the Word. And this attitude
which we inculcate into our lives by the regular practice of
centering prayer does indeed spread out through the rest
of our lives.

Not only do we stop running up and down the path of life for twenty minutes twice a day. We begin to walk along life's way with a certain presence, always listening, always open to the Word of the Lord as he speaks to us in the events of the day, in the persons we encounter, in all the beauties of his creation.

As the truth takes hold in us, its roots pulverize the prejudices. And we are happy to see them go. The perception of our true self, that beautiful image of God now perceived in the eyes of God, frees us from the false identity that had such a pernicious hold on us. We don't have to do or to have now. We are. And we are magnificent; we are the beloved of God. The clutching thorns are gone.

But what makes the difference? Why does one produce a hundredfold, another sixty, another thirty?

There is something more than listening/hearing: "And the seed sown in rich soil is someone who hears the word *and understands it.*"

The soil is not just open, free from rock and thorn; it also needs to be a rich soil. All open soil will bear fruit. But according to its richness will be the richness of its fruit. The soil of our minds and hearts is enriched by the grace of God; understanding is one of the gifts of the Holy Spirit.

It is gift: "To you is granted to understand the mysteries of the kingdom of Heaven, but to them it is not granted." The fact is that God gives more to some than to others.

Something in our American spirit cries, "That's not fair." The fact of it is, God is not fair. He is completely and perfectly just. We all get our desserts and a whole lot more. We all get the agreed day's wage. But he who is good gives it even to the eleventh-hour worker. When he sets us up—gratuitously, let us remember—he does give some ten talents and some five and some one. We have all already gotten more than we deserve. He is the Lord and Master and can give his grace when and where and how he likes—and *he does*.

However, he who is completely true has also said, "Ask and you shall receive." We can always ask for more. If we don't have all we want, the fact is that we haven't really asked for it. Really asked. God does not listen to lips, he listens to hearts, to the steadfast will, to the intent. Saint James tells us that if we have not received what we have asked for, it is because we are like the waves of the sea, fluctuating this way and that. Too easily do we get caught up with other wants and desires. We're back to the thorns again, but now it is the winds of the sea—our alien desires tossing us about.

When we sit down regularly to our centering, and during that centering, every time we become aware of anything else, we faithfully return to the Lord, gently using our love word, we begin to be steadfast in our intent. And what begins by fidelity to the prayer and in the prayer spreads out to the rest of our lives. Our whole heart's desire is for the Lord. We are a good soil that is constantly asking for the enrichment of his grace.

Understanding is one of the gifts of the Holy Spirit. It is actually an ability that was given us at baptism to see what is "standing under," to perceive God and his loving activity in and through all that is. It is an ability that is activated only by her activity. And the Holy Spirit will act in us only if we graciously give her the space. In centering, we learn how to leave aside all our rational activity and open the space for the activity of the Holy Spirit. Once we have shown the Spirit that we do indeed want her to be active in our lives, then indeed she will act. And not just in the time of prayer. We will begin by her activity to understand all the expressions of the Word in our lives. We will not only listen; we will hear and understand. We will be a constant listening for the divine.

Ultimately the only thing that limits the yield in our lives, the yield of all those wonderful fruits of the Holy Spirit— love, joy, peace, patience, kindness—is ourselves. We don't often speak of the virtue of hope. It is almost a forgotten virtue. And that is where the trouble lies. Our greatest sin is that we expect too little of ourselves because we expect too little of God. We do not have hope. We do not expect great things of God. Said she who was wide open to God and received the greatest of all his surprises, "He that is mighty has done great things for me. And his mercy is from generation to generation, to those who reverence him." We hope for little because we have so little sense of his immense goodness, his intense love, his very intimate love for each of us individually and personally. Again, it is in sitting in the silence, listening with our whole being, that we get in touch with his presence and his active creative love deep within our very being. Once we begin to get in touch with this, we begin to expect all things of him. Our desire grows. Our hope grows. Our expectations grow. We don't so much ask as become an asking and therefore constant. And so we are ever growing, like an interest-bearing account whose interest gains are constantly added to the capital. "Anyone who has will be given more and will have more than enough."

Again I will say it: I am in awe at how such a little practice as centering prayer—sitting in the silence for twenty minutes twice a day, longing in love—can have such an immense impact on our lives. Some things are known only by experience. And this is one of them. Do it and see. "Anyone who has ears should listen!"

Chapter 20

✤

The Gift of Centering Prayer

The disciples went up to Jesus and asked, "Why do you talk to them in parables?" In answer, he said, "Because to you is granted to understand the mysteries of the kingdom of Heaven, but to them it is not granted. Anyone who has will be given more and will have more than enough; but anyone who has not will be deprived even of what he has. The reason I talk to them in parables is that they look without seeing and listen without hearing or understanding. So in their case what was spoken by the prophet Isaiah is being fulfilled:

> Listen and listen, but never understand!
> Look and look, but never perceive!
> This people's heart has grown coarse,
> their ears dulled, they have shut their eyes tight
> to avoid using their eyes to see, their ears to hear,
> their heart to understand,
> changing their ways and being healed by me.

"But blessed are your eyes because they see, your ears because they hear! In truth I tell you, many prophets and upright people longed to see what you see, and

never saw it; to hear what you hear, and never heard
it."

Matthew 13:10–17

"Why do you talk to them in parables?" In our centering
prayer we might ask the Lord, "Why do you speak to us
by silence?"

Part of the answer is God's immense reverence for us.
He does not want to overwhelm us or force us by the
cogency of his arguments, the clarity of his truth. He
gently offers the gift of his truth to us, offers himself to us,
in such a way that our freedom remains intact. We are free
to choose to respond to him in faith and love or to go our
own way, following our own lights.

There is another reason, though. No words can adequately express what God is seeking to express to us: his
immense, all-embracing, creative love for us. What can he
say, what could anyone say that would adequately express
love? Story, song, symbol, poetry can perhaps be a vehicle
that tells something and at the same time makes it clear
that there is so much more and invites us to reach beyond
the words toward that so much more.

This revelation is a gift, given freely by God to whom he
pleases. Like any other gift, it needs to be accepted. A gift
is truly accepted when the recipient not only takes the gift
in hand but actually makes use of it in his or her life. We
have all probably had the experience of having someone
accept a gift from us, and perhaps even express all sorts of
appreciation, but then tuck it away never to use it. Such a
gift was never really accepted. It will make no contribution
to the life of the recipient. When one does really accept a

gift and lets it make the contribution it can to his or her life, then the one "who has will be given more and will have more than enough." He will not only have the gift, but he will experience the joy of receiving, the affirmation of his worth, the new sharing in the life of the other, and all the enrichments the gift itself can bring into his life.

All the wonderful truths of the Christian faith are gifts, freely given to us. The truth is there is more than we will ever be able to fully receive in a lifetime. How rich, enriched, and enriching our lives can be if we do spend our time as fully as possible receiving as fully as possible the gifts the Lord is lavishing upon us in the revelation of his life and love, his plan and his providence.

But alas, we do have sluggish hearts. The great spiritual fathers of old used to warn their disciples especially against the vice of *acedia,* a certain spiritual laziness, a lassitude, a lack of energy and enthusiasm in our response to God and the things of God. They considered it one of the basic vices, if not the most basic vice that besets us.

We stand week after week, or even day after day, in the Eucharistic assembly and hear the words of the Good News. We sit with our Bible and listen to the Word of the Lord. Brothers and sisters speak to us of the things of the Lord. And they are scarcely heard. Really heard. They remain just so much information instead of bringing about in us formation or a true reformation. Yes, we *listen and listen but never understand* (hear what is really being conveyed under the words); we *look and look, but never perceive.*

We are all seeking happiness. And we know that heaven means happiness. The Lord has said to us many times, "The kingdom of Heaven is within." And yet . . .

Why are we so loath to go within? Why do we want to cling to the outward things, the things we can see with these physical eyes or with our rational intellect. Much of the time in Scripture, Jesus speaks to us about the kingdom of heaven in parables. And we *listen without hearing or understanding.* We do not know what is to our peace and happiness.

This is one of the reasons why we need to support our practice of centering prayer with those things that will increase and build up our faith. We need our daily *lectio* where we hear the Word of God. For *faith comes through hearing.* We need to form support groups or call others forth to center with us. Not only are we supported then by the accountability that comes with this, but we are also strengthened in our faith by the witness of their faith.

When we center regularly, the inner eyes of faith begin to open up. Through the activity of the Holy Spirit in his gifts we begin to understand. Like Saint Paul, we can say, "I know in whom I believe."

And then the Lord says to us, "Blessed are your eyes because they see, your ears because they hear!"

Obviously the Lord is not here speaking of the fact that the disciples could see him then and there with the physical eyes of their body. That was indeed a blessing, but one much abused. Everyone standing around him, the multitudes who rushed to him, all could see with their physical eyes. So could the Pharisees and Sadducees. But *look and look, they never perceived.* It is the perception of the inner eye of faith that is the blessing, the hearing that understands, a gift from on high. As Jesus said to Saint Peter on another occasion, "Blessed are you, Simon, son of Jonah, because flesh and blood has not revealed this to you, but my Father in Heaven."

It is when we go within, into that kingdom of heaven that is within, when we enter the cloud of unknowing (unknowing as far as the rational intellect can perceive) that we effectively hear the Father say to us, "This is my Son, my Beloved. Listen to him." In centering prayer we listen and listen and we do understand, through the activity of the Holy Spirit in the gifts. We look and look, and in a new way we perceive ourselves—as we are seen in the eyes of God—God himself, and every other person. Indeed, the whole of creation is perceived in a new way, as shot through with divinity. Then, indeed, *blessed are our eyes.* For we have what every upright person longs to see. Our hearts do understand, we change our ways, and we are fully healed.

Centering prayer is a great blessing, a way to even more blessings. Not every one has been granted this gift. If it has been given to you, truly accept it. Use it well and let it enrich your life.

Chapter 21

❖

Let the Darn Darnel Be

Jesus put another parable before them. "The kingdom of Heaven may be compared to a man who
sowed good seed in his field. While everybody was
asleep his enemy came, sowed darnel all among the
wheat, and made off. When the new wheat sprouted
and ripened, then the darnel appeared as well. The
owner's laborers went to him and said, 'Sir, was it
not good seed that you sowed in your field? If so,
where does the darnel come from?' He said to them,
'Some enemy has done this.' And the laborers said,
'Do you want us to go and weed it out?' But he said,
'No, because when you weed out the darnel you
might pull up the wheat with it. Let them both grow
till the harvest, and at harvest time I shall say to the
reapers: First collect the darnel and tie it in bundles
to be burnt, then gather the wheat into my barn.' "

Matthew 13:24–30

In order to center well, it is important that we sow good
seed. As Jesus tells us elsewhere, the seed is the Word of
God.

Centering prayer depends on faith. We can not love what we do not know. It is through faith that we come to know God in any deep and personal way and thus are able to love him. "Faith," as Saint Paul tells us, "comes through hearing," hearing the Word of God. Thus, the way we nurture our centering prayer is to nurture our faith, and the way we nurture our faith is by sacred reading, sowing deep within our minds and our hearts the precious Word of God. This we do by *lectio divina.*

If we want to be faithful to our practice of centering prayer and grow in it, we will take time each day to sow the good seed in our hearts. We will set aside a time, even if it be a very small amount of time, to sit with the Word. There are some things that can help us to plant it well:

1. When we come to our *lectio,* let us be very conscious that the Lord himself is present and alive in his Word. We are not just reading some words; we are coming into his presence to listen to him.

2. Call upon the Holy Spirit to help us in the planting. It was she who planted and nurtured the Word in the mind and heart of the sacred writer and made it come forth for our seeding.

3. Listen! Really listen. Let the Lord speak to us. Try to be a wide-open listening so that he can stretch the parameters of our listening and re-create us more to his own dimensions.

4. Take time. Even if it is only five or ten minutes. Really take the time and give the Lord the whole of our attention. No rush. It is better to hear one word deeply, in a transforming way, than to collect a lot of words and information that is superficial and will probably be blown away before it can ever bear the fruit of faith.

5. In that same spirit, at the end of our time, let us choose one particular word to carry away with us. It may really represent a phrase or a whole sentence or paragraph. But let it be a word of life for us. Something we can nurture through the day, planting it ever more deeply so that it can grow in us forever, a source of constant faithfulness.

6. And do all with a spirit of gratitude. When we are grateful, it means we appreciate what we are receiving, cherish it more fully, and are less apt to let it be dissipated.

The more good seed we pack into our little plot, the less room there is going to be for that darn darnel. But no matter how tightly we pack in the good seed, the false self is always there to sow the other. Our centering will always be sown over with thoughts, images, feelings, and emotions that have nothing to do with the prayer and threaten to sap some of its vitality.

We can have some very negative feelings about the enemy's darnel. When I first started practicing centering prayer, I used to have an exhausting time. I was using my prayer word like a vigorously wielded hoe, trying to cut out at the roots all those weedy thoughts. That's not the way to handle the situation. As the author of *The Cloud of Unknowing* says, "Be careful in this work and never strain your mind or imagination, for truly you will not succeed in this way. Leave these faculties at peace." We just let them, with all their thoughts and images, go on as they will. Otherwise, paying attention to them, trying to handle the weedy thoughts and images, we will not be able to pay attention to God, to the direction of our word of faith. If we begin to try to weed out the stray thoughts, we will have no thought of God, we will be all taken up with our project; a field without weeds, a mind without any thoughts will become our goal. And we will have succeeded even more effectively than the weeds to destroy our prayer.

Let me give you a rather simplistic illustration. Suppose two men are standing near a window on the fourth floor of a building engaged in a very serious and important exchange. (What can be more serious or important than the deep loving exchange we are having with the Lord in centering?) There develops a great commotion down below on the street which draws their attention and interrupts their conversation. Instead of just gently moving away from the window and keeping the exchange going, one of the men races down the three flights of stairs, rushes out into the street, and vainly attempts to quiet all the people who are causing the commotion, leaving his interlocutor up on the fourth floor. Who has really done the exchange in?

When we become aware of those darn(el) thoughts, let us follow the directive of the Owner and simply leave them alone. Let us gently keep our attention on the Owner, our true owner, indeed. He constantly keeps watch on the situation. And when the time is ripe and the crop is ripe, he will see that the good fruit of our centering is harvested and the rest is properly disposed of.

Actually, he who sees to it that *for those who love God all things work together unto good,* uses the weedy thoughts and images even while the wheat is growing. The Owner uses the weeds to loosen the soil to facilitate the growth of the good plantings. The thoughts and images, if we just let them go, take away with themselves the tensions that have been stored up within us and have cramped our freedom.

And so, we just sit quietly in our prayer of centering, confident that when the time of harvest comes, the Master will reap out of our lives all that he wants. There will be wheat aplenty to gather into his barns.

Wheat is gathered into barns for two purposes. Much of it will be used to nourish life. First of all, the life of the owner and then the lives of others. We are the first to be nurtured by our centering. But our prayer has a natural overflow of grace and life that flows through the whole of the Body of Christ, nourishing every part. The good farmer also stores his wheat in order to be able to seed new fields. As our experience and understanding and zeal grows, we are able to share the prayer itself, teaching others how to tend their inner fields, sowing good seed, leaving the darnel be, and attaining a rich harvest for the Owner and for us all.

Anyone who has actually engaged in farming knows how much patience it all takes. Not only is there a temptation to pull up the weeds as soon as they appear. There is the long wait for anything at all to appear. And then there are the long dog days of summer when nothing seems to be making any progress at all. Centering prayer is just like that. At first we can see little fruit for our hours of quiet sitting, day after day. And even after we have had the gratifying experience of actually discerning some promising fruit in our lives and have learned to let the darnel be for now, there are the dog days, when absolutely nothing seems to be happening. We are just waiting. It is a good thing that one of the fruits of the Spirit, those fruits she so

stealthily nurtures within us when we give her the opening, is the fruit called patience.

Old Father Edmund, whom I have already mentioned,
used to quote to me that word of Scripture: "Patience hath
a perfect work." A patience born of faith and hope and
love, nurtured in us by the Spirit who is Love, will enable
us to daily sit in the silence waiting, knowing that good
seed has been sown; that the weeds will not prevent its
growth; that in due time, when we have fully matured, the
Owner will see us safely into his barn; and that our lives
will be fruitful and will nurture and give birth to new life.
We have but to be faithful, remain rooted through daily
practice, and be patient with ourselves and with our
Owner.

Chapter 22

Smallest of All

Jesus put another parable before them, "The kingdom of Heaven is like a mustard seed which a man took and sowed in his field. It is the smallest of all the seeds, but when it has grown it is the biggest of shrubs and becomes a tree, so that the birds of the air can come and shelter in its branches."

Matthew 13:31–32

Have you ever seen a mustard seed, held one in your hand? It is small indeed, smaller than a radish seed.

Centering prayer is like that—very small indeed. When you get down to it, the practice, precisely as practice, is made up of one single little word. "A simple word, a single-syllable word is best," to quote the author of *The Cloud of Unknowing*.

Our oldest historical record of this way of prayer comes from the early desert tradition. A young westerner, John Cassian by name, had gone in search of true wisdom. He traveled far visiting all the strongholds of ancient Christian tradition. He approached all the great masters he could

find, the spiritual fathers and mothers. It was in the far-
thest reaches of Egypt, in ancient Scete, that he found a
man reputed to be the holiest, oldest and wisest father of
the desert. To him John addressed his most basic question: "Father, give me a word on prayer. How do you
pray?" When John returned to the father a second time
with the same question, thus convincing the elder of his
sincerity, Abba Isaac imparted to the young seeker the
teaching which we now capsulate in the centering prayer
method. As he did so, the father extolled the value of
being content with "the poverty of a single word."

That is centering prayer, a very simple, poverty-stricken
method, having only a word. Very little indeed in compari-
son to a rosary or the divine office or the full richness of a
Eucharistic liturgy. It is the smallest of all.

It certainly does not involve any feats of intellect, imagination, or memory. In fact, these are to be left completely
out of it. Again, as the author of *The Cloud of Unknowing*
says, "Be careful in this work and never strain your mind
or imagination, for truly you will not succeed in this way.
Leave these faculties at peace."

Centering prayer is just a simple little word of love.
And, to quote *The Cloud* again, "It is best when this word
is wholly interior without a definite or actual sound."

Little though it is, centering prayer can become "the
biggest." It can have an enormous effect in our lives and
in the lives of others.

It can spread out its branches wide. Centering prayer is
one of the easiest ways for us to move toward constant
prayer, fulfilling the command of the Lord and the admo-
nition of Saint Paul to "pray without ceasing." As the
prayer word becomes more and more ours through regular

practice, we will find that it begins to be present spontaneously at other times. We are walking down the street, waiting for an elevator, doing the dishes, and suddenly the prayer word is there, drawing us for a moment into the depths to enjoy the intimate embrace of the Lord. We wake up in the morning and the word is there and we realize that we have been praying with it all through the night. "I sleep, but my heart watches."

Our love word becomes a real ally in the struggle to live a truly Christian life. Through continued use, this little word develops a natural facility to carry us into the depths. So when we are molested by thoughts and feelings we do not want—angry thoughts, depressing thoughts, lusty feelings—instead of struggling with them, which often serves only to build up their strength, we can turn to our little word and go to the depths. As we do, the unwanted thought or feeling will quite naturally float away. If it is something that has a strong hold on us, then we might have to rest for a bit within, using the word until the unwanted loses its grip.

More important than these blessings and more radical is the fact that this simple prayer opens within us the space for the Holy Spirit to work through her gifts. When through her influence and operation the divine instinct grows in us, we find that we are indeed able to pray constantly. While at one level we are attending to our daily affairs, giving our mind and heart to what is at hand, at a deeper level we are aware of God in all that we are doing and each person we are encountering and our heart is adoring and loving and praising and thanking. We perceive God in all and all in God. We therefore have a caring reverence, a loving respect for each person and each thing that he is bringing forth in his creative love, abiding in his providential care, and enriching our lives with his fatherly friendship.

There comes about in our lives a true transformation of consciousness. This is not just a matter of new and wonderful insights, though these do come. Nor is it a matter of moral correctness, though coming to love God more deeply and intimately, we do seek more faithfully to keep his commandments. There may be good feelings, consolations of a high order. There will be a certain deep peace and joy—all those fruits of the Spirit.

But above all there will be an enormous expansion of heart and a growth in compassion, *so that the birds of the air can come and shelter in our branches.* We will become a place of refuge, a home for the homeless, a safe harbor for those who sense themselves tossed about with doubt and fear and trouble. This is a most necessary fruit if we are to be truly one with Christ and his Church in their option for the poor.

I have already related how the little seed of centering prayer has developed into the great shrubs and trees of Food for the Poor and S.H.A.R.E. I could tell many other stories. I could tell you about Janet, who lives at Mary House in New York, a home for shopping-bag ladies. Each month my copy of the *Catholic Worker* arrives with the caption HUGS FROM THE HUGGER. The hugs of this Hugger, as we affectionately call Janet, reach out to affirm and console hundreds across the nation. Then there is Conchitina Bernardo. This wealthy matron never had to do anything but govern her household of servants. Then the prayer entered into her life. Today, as vice-mayor of Makati, a Manila suburb, she spends many hours in the miserable alleyways of the worst sort of slums, listening to the needs of the people and doing something about them. I shall never lose the image of this delicate, charming woman deftly avoiding the refuse and muck as she led me among the hovels of one of her slums, dispensing her compassionate love in all directions.

These wonderful Christians, in the way they live for others, poor impoverished strangers whom they recognize as sisters and brothers, as Christ himself, and effectively care for them—these women and men are making the kingdom of heaven present in our world today. The kingdom of heaven is like centering prayer which these women and men have sowed in their fields. It has grown, it is the biggest of shrubs and becomes a tree, so that the needy can come and shelter in its branches.

For centering prayer to produce these results, it must be *sowed in our field.* We must make it a part of our life. Regularly, at least twice a day, if we are going to be able to support vast undertakings, to be there in compassion for the many, we are going to need to rest deeply in the Lord and get in touch with the true source of our vision and our energy, our courage and our pertinacity. Only when centering prayer is sown deeply into our lives can we expect that it will become the biggest, providing a place of refuge for those who fly about seeking a place of rest. Only if we faithfully abide in prayer can we hope to be a credible sign of the kingdom of heaven and effectively make it present.

Chapter 23

❖

Yeast

Jesus told them another parable, "The kingdom of Heaven is like yeast a woman took and mixed in with three measures of flour till it was leavened all through."

In all this Jesus spoke to the crowds in parables; indeed, he would never speak to them except in parables. This was to fulfill what was spoken by the prophet:

> *I will speak to you in parables,*
> *unfold what has been hidden since the foundation*
> *of the world.*

> *Matthew 13:33–35*

Anyone who has practiced centering prayer for some time will readily tell you it is indeed yeast. It leavens our whole life, every aspect of it.

We could consider the three measures the three states of consciousness: waking, sleeping, and dreaming. Centering prayer brings us into a fourth state of consciousness. We might call it transcendental consciousness or God con-

sciousness. Once it has begun to develop in our lives, it
can coexist with any one of the other three states and
enliven them. It is that level of consciousness on which
the Holy Spirit works in us through her gifts. While our
waking consciousness is busy about many things, this
deeper consciousness can be sitting at the Lord's feet, perceiving him in everything and everyone, and worshipping.
While we are sleeping, this consciousness can still be
watchful and in prayer. As the wise man wrote in that
song of divine love, the Song of Songs, "I sleep but my
heart watches." We begin to pray day and night. And
when dreams come to us in the night, this consciousness
is aware of the presence and message of God in them.

All the levels of our consciousness are enriched and
enlivened by the state of consciousness we come to when
we willingly lay aside our human reasoning and open ourselves to the activity of the Holy Spirit through her gifts.

We might also see the three measures as three faculties
in the human person: the intellect, the will, and the emotions. Centering prayer has a profound effect on the activity of each of these three.

In general, when we center regularly, the intellect operates much better. We learn to be all there. And wide open.
Our prejudices, competitiveness, and defensiveness have
been dissipated. When our interest in our false self dwin-
dles and dies, we don't have to keep an eye on ourselves
any longer. We can look with both eyes and listen with
both ears. We see more, hear more, are more fully present
to the sources of knowledge and information. We learn
more, more quickly. At the same time, having opened to
the activity of the Holy Spirit, we find new depths of
knowledge and understanding are available to us through

the activity of her gifts. The intellect is much more enlightened and satisfied.

The will, too, is more empowered and satisfied. Seeing God more fully, his immense goodness and beauty, we are drawn more powerfully to him in love. With fuller knowledge the will is less apt to be drawn away after the passing goods of this world. Our love is more steadfast and deep. We are less apt to stray. We stand up better in the face of temptation.

This deeper, richer knowledge and love set free our emotions, and our feelings flow more freely and fully. Those who have long trodden the ways of active purgation are often surprised by this. They have learned to be suspicious of feelings and emotions. They often fear them and seek to ignore them, if not suppress them. But with a new sense of our own goodness and the goodness of others, we rejoice that we are able to express this goodness on every level of our being and respond to it in others. There is new space for love.

Many married couples have told me how centering prayer has freed them to be more fully to each other in love. Centering together seems at times to create a communion more deep and complete than that of the marital embrace. I think here of a particular couple who had been married many years. Prior to their meeting he had been a religious priest and she had been a religious woman. Both had discerned a call to new ministries and had left their earlier vocations. Later they met and entered into the sacrament of matrimony. Their life together was rich and full, bringing wonderful services to the Christ-community. But in their expression of their mutual love, they always experienced a certain holding back. It was only when they began to center that they found the freedom to give themselves fully to each other and enjoy to the full the most intimate expressions of marital love.

Again we can see the three measures being leavened by centering prayer as the mind, body, and spirit.

Some of the masters who have been teaching different forms of Eastern meditation in the West have strongly extolled the psychological and physical benefits that accrue from the regular practice of meditation. These are very real. In fact, I do not know how anyone can survive well without a regular practice of meditation. Our atmosphere is so charged with all sorts of frenetic energy. We are constantly coming under different forms of stress and strain. The effects of this stress and strain are stored up first of all in our minds but then also in our bodies. If we do not have some way of releasing them, they will eventually take their toll in psychological and physiological problems.

Meditation releases stress. As we sit quietly in centering prayer, resting in the depths with the Lord, our mind continues to operate. Thoughts and images flow along. If they are allowed to flow freely, the stress that surrounds them flows away with them. Sometimes we might have a rather striking experience of some old memory coming up, and as we let it go, there goes with it whole areas of tension in our human relations. One young man shared with me how an early memory of a very painful experience came up for him during his meditation. As he let it go, all the anger he had long been harboring toward his father went with it. At other times, we might experience the sudden release of knots of tension that have long been stored in our bodies. I have heard many remarkable stories. But most of the time the healing goes on very quietly. The daily tensions are released before they can be stored, and old ones dissolve bit by bit. Only gradually do we become aware of the difference. We begin to handle relationships better. We enjoy things more, the little things of life, the basic things —sound, color, images. Our creative energies seem to function more freely. Others note a softening of our features. We look younger. There is a sparkle in our eyes. All in all, life seems very good. At the root of this is the leavening of the spirit. We come to know who we are, how loved we are, who this God of love is. Life flows up powerfully and freely from within, from the very Source of life who is ever present at the center of our being, with all his creative love.

As we sit in centering prayer, things do become clearer. It is not so much that we have brilliant insights; indeed, during the time of prayer we let all these things go. But there grows in us a deep sense that life does make sense. There is a certain unfolding. What has been hidden from us, the missing pieces of the puzzle of life seem to show up. It is leavened all through. Something of the completeness, the allness, the peace of heaven begins to be present. God is at the center of our being. We let him truly be the Lord and Master of our domain. The kingdom of God is established within.

All of this is the wonderful fruit of centering prayer. Yet let me utter a word of caution. We must not go to the prayer seeking any of these things. If we do, we can very easily turn the prayer into something else. It can be a self seeking, another project of the false self. For the prayer to be what it is, and thus able to bear these fruits, we must come to it seeking only God. The prayer must ever be gift

—love is not love until it is given away—a pure gift of ourselves to God. In giving ourselves to him, becoming truly his, we allow him to do with us freely whatever he wants. And he who made us to share his happiness will surely see that that is precisely what comes about. Fully and freely sharing the happiness of God—is that not what heaven is? Centering prayer is of heaven because it brings all the facets of our being, all the levels of our consciousness, to fulfillment, peace, and happiness.

Chapter 24

A Treasure, a Pearl,
a Dragnet

The kingdom of Heaven is like treasure hidden in a
field which someone has found; he hides it again,
goes off in his joy, sells everything he owns and buys
the field.

Again, the kingdom of Heaven is like a merchant
looking for fine pearls; when he finds one of great
value he goes and sells everything he owns and buys
it.

Again, the kingdom of Heaven is like a dragnet
that is cast in the sea and brings in a haul of all kinds
of fish. When it is full, the fishermen haul it ashore;
then, sitting down, they collect the good ones in baskets and throw away those that are no use.

Matthew 13:44–48

Do you remember when you first discovered centering
prayer? It was a wonderful moment, wasn't it? You had
found a treasure, a pearl of great worth.

But quickly enough you learned that in order to possess this inner kingdom, you did indeed have to sell all you possessed. When we "possess" something, grasp it to ourselves as ours, rather than our possessing it we discover that in fact it possesses us. It makes a constant claim on us: care, attention, worry, fear that we might lose it or it might suffer some damage. When we are very much into the false self, which is constituted of what we have or possess, as well as what we can do (in order to possess more) and what others think of us (usually according to what we possess), possessing things becomes even more important. What we possess is seen as our very self. Hanging on to what we possess becomes a matter of life and death.

Coming to centering prayer, we learn that we must give up all that we possess, let go of all the binding limitations these place upon us, or we can never have the openness and freedom of the kingdom. To be free to possess the inner kingdom, we must give up everything that we hold in a possessive way. Not only our exterior goods, our abilities, what others think of us, but even those more intimate possessions—our thoughts and feelings. We must *sell everything we own,* everything we hold with a sense of ownership, so that we can freely enter into possession of the kingdom of heaven.

If we "possess" our feelings and emotions, our assessments and judgments, then they, like our material possessions, indeed possess us. They push us around, they make demands on us, they inhibit our freedom. If we need to have certain reassuring feelings, we get very involved in the self in seeking to bring forth these. We are not free to let things be as they are and respond in simple faith to the deep reality of the kingdom within us. If our perspective is limited by our assessments and judgments, so that we are a narrow listening, able only to hear what falls within our established limits, the full reality of the kingdom can find no space within us.

When we do "sell everything," we do find a wonderful freedom. A great space opens within us. And if we enter with faith we discover that there has indeed been a treasure hidden in our field, the very kingdom of heaven. That pearl of great value, centering prayer, enables us to enter into that kingdom anytime we are willing to sell everything we own to buy it.

When we practice centering prayer, though, we discover it is not only the kingdom of heaven, a beautiful place wherein we can rest in the divine presence and be refreshed and renewed. It is also a dragnet. It brings up all sorts of things from the deep seas within. Good and bad thoughts, memories of old and wild new imaginings, very useful insights and painful ones, the garbage and the treasures emerge. This is natural. This is good. God uses this surfacing to release, by a natural healing process, the tensions that have become lodged in our psyche and our bodies. The important thing for us is that during the process, during our time of centering, we allow the Lord to work freely with his dragnet. We let the stuff surface and float away. We don't get involved in trying to see what is there, and even more so we don't try to collect some of the catch. No, during the time of the prayer we attend to the Lord. It is his dragnet; we let him use it as he will.

"When it is full," when we have completed our time, then we can haul it ashore and perhaps do some sorting out. This is not necessary. It certainly is not a part of the

centering prayer as such. But sometimes it can be profit-
able. The danger is that if we go to the prayer with this
intention, we will be strongly tempted to begin the sorting
during the prayer, interfering with the process itself. Or
worse, rather than the prayer being what it is, a pure and
total gift of self to the Lord, our prayer becomes vitiated by
our coming to it seeking something for ourselves.

Actually, what I have found in practice is this: if there is
anything of worth caught up in the dragnet, if there is
creative and productive thought achieved by the mind
while we center, or if past memories worth reconsidera-
tion do emerge, or anything like that, and if we faithfully
let them go during the prayer, to choose simply God, after-
ward they will come back and be there for us. By letting
them go during the prayer, they have been freed of the
tensions that surround them. When we later meet them,
we have a freedom and clarity to work fully with them.

I know there is a special temptation for preachers and
writers (since I am one of them) to want to grab onto the
wonderful thoughts that sometimes emerge in the prayer. I
see this as the Lord playing with us, saying in effect, "Do
you love me more than this?" We are willing to let these
little treasures go in order to have the treasure, our Lord
himself, and his kingdom of light and peace and love.
This I know from experience: if we do succumb to the
temptation and grab hold of a particular line of thought or
an insight during the prayer, we will later find it is only
"half-baked." It isn't all there. But if we let go of it—put it
back in the oven—later we will be able to find it and it
will be "well-done," ready for us to enjoy and to serve up
to others.

So "when it is full," when the time allotted for our

centering prayer is complete, then, and only then, might we collect the good ones.

"And throw away those that are no use." Sometimes beginners are shocked with the thoughts and images that surface during their prayer. We do not need to be shocked by anything. When we are centering, our minds and imaginations are set free to run where they will, as they are in the dreaming state. Anything at all might come up, from the actual past or from the fabrications of a fertile imagination. No matter. In every case during the prayer we simply let them go. They can be cleaning out a lot of muck and all the tension surrounding it. This is good. Let it be. Let God go about his healing work within us. After the prayer, if some of the less useful thoughts or images reoccur, we will find that we can more easily let go of them because in letting go of them during the centering prayer, the tensions around them and the hold they have on us have been greatly weakened, if not totally released. We can simply "throw away those that are no use."

Yes, centering prayer is a treasure. It opens the way for us to enter the kingdom of heaven. In its fullness, it is that kingdom, already experienced here on the journey, experienced in faith. It might also give us a catch of good thoughts, feelings, resolutions. These are only secondary and accidental. All of this will be so, though, only if we are willing to sell everything, to become completely dispossessed, for it is to the poor in spirit that the kingdom of heaven belongs.

Chapter 25

❖

You Can't Lose

When Jesus had finished these parables he left the
district, and coming to his home town, he taught the
people in their synagogue in such a way that they
were astonished and said, "Where did the man get
this wisdom and these miraculous powers? This is
the carpenter's son, surely? Is not his mother the
woman called Mary, and his brothers James and Joseph and Simon and Jude? His sisters, too, are they
not all here with us? So where did the man get it all?"
And they would not accept him. But Jesus said to
them, "A prophet is despised only in his own country and in his own house." And he did not work
many miracles there because of their lack of faith.

Matthew 13:53–58

When we first discover centering prayer, there is often,
though not always, a tremendous joy. It opens such wonderful space in our lives. We are then quite naturally eager
to share this newfound treasure, this pearl of great worth,
with those whom we most love, with our own family, with

our intimate friends, with our neighbors and our parish.
But we will have our hesitancies. The gospel narrative of
Jesus' return to Nazareth will quickly come to mind.

I would like here to urge you to let go by those thoughts
and feelings that incline you to hesitate, just as you let go
the thoughts and feelings that arise in the centering prayer
itself. Let them go, and courageously and lovingly share
your new treasure.

As we have already noted a number of times, centering
prayer opens space, welcoming the Holy Spirit to act in us
through the gifts we received at baptism. Then, as we
begin to share, we will have a wisdom that is not our own.
The Holy Spirit will act in and through us. We will also
have the help of the gift of counsel. If we but gently listen,
the Holy Spirit will guide us into the best way to share
with each person who is in our life or who might come
into it. The gift of understanding will be working too. We
will receive the insights we need to explain the practice
well, in the best way for each particular person or group of
persons. I can say with the greatest of assurance, speaking
from my own experience, that you will often be surprised
at what you are saying and how answers to questions
come to you. If you are faithful to your practice, the Holy
Spirit will not let you down.

The presence and activity of the Spirit will not limit
themselves to the times when you are sharing the centering prayer. Through the activity of the gifts, your whole
life will be enriched and transformed. The change will
perhaps not be so striking that it will cause surprise. A
rather quiet, shy person might well find that he or she is
now clearer and more articulate, more socially inclined
and active. A sad person might find that there is a lot more

joy in life; a worrisome person might find a growing peace. A swinger might settle down to being more faithful. I could give rather interesting examples of all of these.

However, it is when you attempt to share the source of all of this, the centering prayer, that you might encounter the most articulate rebuff. Here perhaps you will need to depend on the Holy Spirit's gifts of fortitude and piety, that persevering and faithful love of family and friends. Here the fruits of the Spirit might be needed—patience, kindness, and long-suffering. Before you are done, you might well be tempted to quote Jesus' words: "A prophet is despised only in his own country and in his own house." Though this is perhaps not the best way to imitate the Master.

Nonetheless, you might find some comfort in knowing that Jesus did share your experience.

Jesus must have arrived at Nazareth with a certain joy in his heart. He had been widely acclaimed everywhere he went. Crowds were seeking after him. He now had a fine group of loyal disciples who supported him in his ministry. Wonderful things had been happening. Now, at last, he was able to bring these blessings to the friends and neighbors with whom he had grown up and for whom he had a special love. He could bring joy to their homes and to their hearts, perhaps returning some of the little kindnesses they had shown to him and his mother over the years. That was his hope as he climbed the steep hill to the little town that nestles high above the plains. But it was a hope that was destined to be dashed to the ground. As one of the Gospels puts it, "he was amazed."

Like so many of us, his people had a particular listening, or rather were a particular listening, a very narrow listening. And there was little inclination to let anything they saw or heard change that listening. For them, Jesus was "the carpenter's son" and carpenters' sons were expected to act in a certain way and know only so much. "Where did he get this wisdom and these miraculous powers?" He is Mary's boy. We know his cousins. They live down the lane and up the hill. He is just one of us, so how can he now teach us anything new, how can he presume to teach about high and lofty things?

And you? You are just somebody's husband or wife, brother or sister, a neighbor. You have long lived here like the rest of us, with the job you have always had. How can you now teach us about prayer—especially about contemplative prayer and transforming union? Who do you think you are?

Hopefully, centering prayer has expanded your own listening, if not yet theirs, and you can quietly respond, at least to yourself, I am the very image of God, God's beloved child, who has received his Spirit in baptism along with all her gifts. "We do not know how to pray as we ought, but the Holy Spirit prays within us." I have come to learn that that is true. Moreover, "the Advocate, the Paraclete, will teach you all things." I need only open the space with my sharing. Quietly, then, and confidently, with full dependence on the Holy Spirit, you will go ahead and share what you have received. "Freely have you received, freely give."

Jesus "did not work many miracles there because of their lack of faith." Not many, but he did work some. He did bring healing to some of those whom he loved.

So, like Jesus, do go to those whom you love, those with whom you live, and open the space for them to rejoice with you and find healing and fuller life. At the same time, know that, perhaps like Jesus, you may find that not many will believe in you. They might question and even mock you. Be conscious of the fact that "failure" or meager or limited results will not be your fault if they are rather to be attributed to "their lack of faith." At the same time, be assured that there will be some "miracles," that there will be some who will believe, who will find the joy of centering prayer, who will find deep healing through the prayer when you share it with them. It may not be easy, but isn't it worth withstanding a bit of mockery, a bit of seeming failure, to make it possible for some of those whom you love to find what you have found in centering prayer? And maybe even a lot more.

If you bring this blessing to only one other, it will be a great blessing. For one thing, it will give you someone to be accountable to—perhaps even someone with whom you can meet, if not daily, at least with some regularity, to join in centering prayer. What a great support that can be to your own fidelity in practice. The one with whom you share the prayer might, with your support and encouragement, go on to share it with others. A whole movement has begun. And you with the Lord are the source.

So don't be afraid of a little "astonishment." The Lord is with you, whatever be your success or your failure. That being so, whether you have success or failure, you can't lose.

Nonetheless, it remains a fact that "a prophet is despised only in his own country and in his own house." In view of this, you might wisely team up with someone else you know who is practicing centering prayer, perhaps someone from the workshop or retreat where you yourself learned it. As the local, you might provide the entry, gather the group, make the introduction, but let your companion, the "honored stranger," do the actual teaching. In the course of the ensuing discussion, you yourself can contribute. And then, with the endorsement of your friend, lead the follow-up. In your turn, you might help your friend, as an honored stranger, to bring the centering prayer to his or her home territory. "A brother who helps a brother is like a walled city," says the wise man of the Scriptures. Teamwork can make it a lot easier and a lot more fun, as well as being more effective.

No matter how you go about sharing and teaching, remember always, it is the Holy Spirit who is the teacher of prayer. Bearing that in mind, don't hesitate to use any opening that comes your way to share the prayer, gently, lovingly, with concern, as something very precious to you. Honest, open, simple sharing can never be offensive. "Faith comes through hearing." Your sharing can be a moment of special grace for someone for whom you care very much. It is worth laying down your life a bit. For "greater love than this no one has than that one lay down one's life for a friend."

If sharing the prayer means being more like Jesus, closer to Jesus, even while you bring a blessing, a way of healing to some who are dear to you, in sharing the prayer, you certainly can't lose.

Chapter 26

Blessed and Broken to Feed Others

When evening came, the disciples went to him and said, "This is a lonely place, and time has slipped by; so send the people away, and they can go to the villages to buy themselves some food." Jesus replied, "There is no need for them to go: give them something to eat yourselves." But they answered, "All we have with us is five loaves and two fish." So he said, "Bring them here to me." He gave orders that the people were to sit down on the grass; then he took the five loaves and the two fish, raised his eyes to heaven and said the blessing. And breaking the loaves he handed them to his disciples, who gave them to the crowds. They all ate as much as they wanted, and they collected the scraps left over, twelve baskets full. Now about five thousand men had eaten, to say nothing of women and children.

Matthew 14:15–22

Time passes us by very quickly at times, or so it seems. And so have the pages of this book. "Time has slipped by."

As we have continued in the practice of our centering prayer, we have become more and more aware of the existence of hunger among our sisters and brothers, a hunger that debilitates and kills. We sense an ever deeper solidarity with each one of them, those found nearby, sad to say, in our own streets in this land so blessed with God's abundance, and those who live far away but are not distanced from us in our common humanity. We sit at our well-stocked tables and know that for many of those who are one with us in Christ, the table—if they have one—is bare. Or there is some meager quantity of rice or gruel or soup that must feed too many little mouths and some big ones too. If our prayer is genuine, we find ourselves doing more and more about this. It is not always easy to know where to draw the line. We have our own responsibilities and needs. But the growing inclination of our heart will be to do ever more.

I was deeply touched recently when a young man told me he was having difficulty knowing how far he should go in responding to the needs of his poor brothers and sisters. I asked him what he was presently doing. With a gentle simplicity he told me how he had been responding to the beggars who approached as long as he had money at all in his pocket, then for the rest of the week he did without, walking to work and fasting. He had given away almost all his furniture and was now sleeping on the floor. He wondered if he should bring some of the homeless into his apartment to share the floor. He had so few clothes left that he had to wash some of them every night for the next day. Few of us will go that far, but we will want to give to the point where it does cost—not just out of our superfluity but out of our substance, as Pope John Paul II urged when he stood in the rain in the streets of New York.

But there is a hunger that is far more acute than the need for bread. There is a deep spiritual hunger. If this spiritual hunger is satisfied, then one can much more easily sustain the pains of physical hunger. But if it is not satisfied, even rich meals never satisfy. It is to this hunger we are called to respond with the nourishing gift of centering prayer.

When we perceive that others around us are hungering for God and a sense of his presence and love in their lives, we are apt to respond like the disciples: "All we have . . ." We look only at what we have, which is always inadequate, forgetting that the Source of what we have, who dwells within us, is the Source of all. We come out of scarcity and need rather than out of creative abundance.

"All we have" is a very little bit of experience, and that is quite confusing. We don't know theology. How could we answer questions? We might lead people astray. So let us send the people away, and they can go to the monasteries to get themselves some teaching.

Whatever it is, whatever we do think we have, it is always much too little, and certainly not adequate. All we have is our five senses, our head, and our heart. How can these poor human tools speak of the divine? What can they know? Our prayer is a jumble of thoughts and feelings. Or, at best, some deep quiet that is beyond anything we can talk about. How can we teach others?

One of the things Jesus says to us in centering prayer is

"Bring them here." Bring me your senses, your mind, your heart. In centering, we bring everything to the Lord, all that we are, all that we have. We give them all to him, to let him do with them what he will. It is he who will heal them and make them whole, make them worthy instruments of the Holy Spirit, who will begin to act in them and through them by means of her gifts.

When we give ourselves with all our faculties to the Lord, he does a number of things with them.

He gives them new direction. He takes them up into his being to the Father. More and more spontaneously do our thoughts and our heart look to heaven.

He blesses our faculties, healing and wholing them. We find a new freedom, power, and integrity. They are more responsive now to the spirit—our spirit. They serve us better. And they are more responsive to the Holy Spirit. They serve her better as instruments through which the gifts can operate, enabling us to operate in a more divine way.

And he breaks them. He breaks open the confining parameters of our listening. Our preconceived ideas, our prejudices, our binding and blinding attachments are all broken. We are ready to be handed over to any and to all of Christ's disciples, no matter how incompatible their race, color, ethnicity, or culture might have previously seemed to us. We are ready to serve in the Church and of the Church, his Body.

As we perceive spiritual hunger—and it is on all sides of us—we are ready to hand out freely what little we have. And surprise: everyone seems to be getting what they want! Sometimes they seem to be getting much more than we have. We are faithfully centering, sitting in the darkness, waiting, hoping, longing, believing. And this person with whom we have just shared the prayer is not only rapt to the seventh heaven, but is out sharing the prayer with everybody in sight and getting groups going and the like. One of the things that clearly comes home to us when we begin to share is the fact that it is not we who do it. "Faith comes through hearing." *Through hearing,* but not from our speaking. Rather, from the Spirit who gets the space she wants through our speaking and the opening that that engenders in the other to listen.

Another thing that may well surprise us when we first begin to share is how much more we ourselves have after we have shared.

One of the things we find we have collected is a lot of support for our own fidelity in practice. Most of us are not quite hypocritical enough to preach to others while we ourselves are not practicing. We experience a certain amount of accountability, which shows up especially in our ongoing sharing. Often, too, there comes out of our sharing the opportunity to form a group that will meet with some regularity. This is tremendously supportive.

We will find also in regards to centering prayer that the old adage certainly holds true: the best way to learn something is to teach it. This is one of the reasons why I always enjoy centering prayer workshops, even though I have led hundreds and hundreds of them over the years. Each time I do, I learn something. I get new insights. People ask new questions. Or the old questions with a slightly different nuances. And new light breaks in. I come away from the teaching not only with a deeper commitment to the prayer but also with a deeper insight into what it means in my life, in the lives of others, and in the life of the Church, the whole Christ. I am most grateful for every opportunity I have to share the prayer.

And I know you will be, too, once you begin to do it. The important thing in this, though, is to bring to Jesus, with the greatest possible fidelity, your five senses, your mind, and your heart, all your feelings, your thoughts, and your desires, your whole being, in your regular practice of centering prayer so that he can redirect them, bless them, and break them open. Then what joy you will have as the divine grace and power flow through you and thousands of men, women, and children are fed and your own inner resources grow and grow.

Chapter 27

❖

To Walk on Water

And at once Jesus made the disciples get into the boat and go on ahead to the other side while he sent the crowds away. After sending the crowds away he went up into the hills by himself to pray. When evening came, he was there alone, while the boat, by now some furlongs from land, was hard pressed by rough waves, for there was a head wind. In the fourth watch of the night he came towards them walking on the sea, and when the disciples saw him walking on the sea they were terrified. "It is a ghost," they said, and cried out in fear. But at once Jesus called out to them, saying, "Courage! It's me! Don't be afraid." It was Peter who answered. "Lord," he said, "if it is you, tell me to come to you across the water." Jesus said, "Come." Then Peter got out of the boat and started walking towards Jesus across the water, but then noticing the wind, he took fright and began to sink. "Lord," he cried, "save me!" Jesus put out his hand at once and held him. "You have so little faith," he said, "why did you doubt?" And as they got into the boat the wind dropped. The men in the boat bowed down before him and said, "Truly, you are the Son of God."

Matthew 14:22–33

Jesus certainly sets us an example here. If the very Son of God needed to go apart to pray, isn't it ridiculous for us to think that we can do the Father's work effectively without going apart regularly to pray?

He sent the crowds away. We can, with a spiritual understanding, see this as Jesus sending away—letting go—of all his thoughts and cares of the day and of his mission, infinitely important though it be, just to rest in the Father. There would be time enough to think about these important things later. Now it was time to be with the Father.

But the literal meaning here is also important for us. Jesus did literally send away the crowds. These were crowds of good and seeking people, people who earnestly wanted and needed his ministry. Nonetheless, he sent them away. It was time for him to pray. He needed to pray. Otherwise he could not continue to do always the things that please the Father; he could not continue to effectively accomplish his ministry, his life's mission. How many good people, especially dedicated priests and religious, say they do not have time to center regularly? There is too much to be done, too many people needing their ministry. And they go on, expecting to accomplish effectively without the refreshment of prayer, what Jesus Christ himself could not accomplish without prayer!

But you can't send needy people away. Jesus did!

Jesus' way of going about things certainly is strange. He came on earth to establish the universal Church, the largest and most powerful and enduring institution in the history of the human race. And what does he do? He spends the first thirty, or more probably thirty-three, years of his life in a quite ordinary way, learning how to live an ordinary prayerful life. When finally he sets forth on his great task, he spends the first forty days in complete retirement, doing nothing but praying. Then he comes forth. He has a power of speech that is unprecedented. And he can work miracles at will. He attracts mobs. Yet, time after time, night after night, he slips away, leaving the clamoring crowds, to spend his time in prayer. But today, his disciples—who rarely hope to do more wonderful things than he did, even though he said they could if they would—can't wait until they are thirty and have had some quiet years to deepen their prayer life before they set forth. No, there is too much to be done and they have to rush out to do it, without ever having taken the time to develop a deep personal communion with the Father, about whose work they are supposed to be. And once they are into that work, they don't have time, not even twenty minutes twice a day, to stop their rushing about to commune with the Father and get deeply in tune with him and his will and open the space for the Spirit to operate within them. Can we really call ourselves disciples of Jesus Christ when we act in a way so different from the way he acted?

"Jesus made the disciples get into the boat." Perhaps the only way some of us will ever seriously set forth on the journey of prayer is if Jesus in some way makes us, if he in some way sends the crowds away from us and puts us out to sea.

And that, of course, is the fact. We embark on the way of centering prayer only if the Lord does get us started, one way or another. We don't always see too clearly that it is he. We might actually think it was only by some coincidence that we came upon the way of centering. As a good Jewish friend of mine says, "You know what a coincidence is? It is God working anonymously." We would never get started on centering prayer if the Lord himself did not get us started.

And it is with his help that we are able to send the crowds away, to let go of the thoughts and feelings and desires that seem to so crowd in on our consciousness. It often, though not always, happens that when we first begin to center, we do receive exceptional help to dismiss these crowds. The Lord gives us a sense, too, that it is all right for us to let him, in his own incomprehensible way, take care of the needs of the needy. Yes, we actually believe that God can take care of his world and his people for twenty minutes without us.

But as time goes on and we continue our journey in centering prayer, seemingly making little or no progress, we begin to feel "hard pressed by rough waves." We need help to persevere on the journey. At this point, the Lord will usually show up in our lives, but in some unexpected guise, one that might be quite frightening. And the challenge will be there to walk on the waters in one way or another. He will give us a courage that is not of this world, the courage that comes from the activity of the Holy Spirit through the gift of fortitude, and then challenge us to step out in faith. It is an invitation to a new kind of oneness with him, to be with him in doing the impossible. How few hear such an invitation. And how many fewer dare to respond.

We are tempted to laugh or at least smile at Peter here.

There he goes again, big-mouth Peter: "Tell me to come to you across the water." And the bravado before the boys in stepping out. And then the true colors show: "Lord, save me!" Maybe we are just laughing at ourselves.

Would that we were! Most of us just have a hard enough time to muster the faith that it takes to stay in the boat of centering prayer when we are "hard pressed by rough waves," and there is a head wind. Managing that, there is hope that the Holy Spirit will in time find the space within us to activate her gifts, and we will discover some courage, the courage of faith, to really listen to the Lord. We know enough from listening to the stories of the saints and seeing what the Father asked of his only Son to know it is a risky thing indeed to really listen for the call of the Lord. His "Come," can indeed mean the ridiculous. Who really wants to walk on water, especially the turbulent waters of a storm-tossed sea. Peter did love the Lord and was drawn by a powerful affection. He did listen. And he heard. And he responded. And he did trust, up to a point. A point most of us never get near.

Jesus Christ does want each one of us to be as closely and fully one with him in his saving mission as we want to be. Yes, he does want us to walk on water, to have a miraculous presence in this world, one that tells of God's power, presence, and tremendous love.

Is there any hope that you and I, so weak, so fearful, so set in duly constituted ways, could ever step out and walk on water?

Yes! If we stay in the boat in spite of the rough waves and the head wind, which means virtually seeing no progress. If we stay there faithfully and let the Lord work in us through the prayer at the pace he knows is best for us, then when he comes walking across the waves to us, we will have the courage the Spirit works in us and be able to recognize him in whatever guise he has chosen. We will have the openness to hear his call and the love to step forth into that sharing of his life and mission to which he beckons us. And if, like Peter, we falter, let us hope that we have the humility of Peter, which enabled him to cry out to his Saviour to be saved.

Even though Peter must have heard Jesus more than once upbraid petitioners for seeking signs, here he himself falls into the same trap. That is undoubtedly why he faltered in the end. "Lord, if it is you . . ." He wanted a sign. He got a sign. But signs don't work. This is one of the things we are slow to learn when in the boat of centering prayer. We keep falling back, trying to judge our prayer by some signs—peace, consolation, good feelings. If we seek reassuring signs in our practice of centering prayer, we will surely falter. For true signs will not—cannot—be given. We will latch on to pseudo signs—feelings of peace, thoughts, images that are actually drawing us away from the prayer. And they will fail us.

This is undoubtedly one of the most difficult things about this very simple form of prayer. It is so pure. It is pure gift, the gift of love. We set out on the journey with no expectations. The boat may move rapidly and smoothly ahead. But it probably won't. We may seem to experience only rough seas—thoughts, feelings, emotions throwing us in every direction. And no progress in the face of terrible head winds. Jesus' presence in our lives may be considerably altered. "We once knew Jesus in the flesh, but we know him so no more." We will be summoned to a more spiritual, "ghostly" relation with him. If we are to be one with him in his universal salvific mission, we must learn to operate on a more lofty spiritual level. In this realm there are no signs that our little human intellect or our all-too-human feelings can latch on to. It is the path above the waters, the way of pure faith and totally trustful love. Tremendously frightening! Tremendously exciting!

This is the possibility. No, more—this is the promise of centering prayer once the Lord has gotten us into the boat. But we do have to be willing to remain faithfully there, sailing ahead, no matter what, by regular faithful practice.

Bon voyage!

Chapter 28

From the Heart

Then Pharisees and scribes from Jerusalem came to Jesus and said, "Why do your disciples break away from the tradition of the elders? They eat without washing their hands." He answered, "And why do you break away from the commandment of God for the sake of your tradition? For God said, *'Honor your father and your mother'* and *'Anyone who curses his father and mother will be put to death.'* But you say, 'If anyone says to his father or mother: Anything I might have used to help you is dedicated to God, he is rid of his duty to father and mother.' In this way you have made God's word ineffective by means of your tradition. Hypocrites! How rightly Isaiah prophesied about you when he said:

> *This people honors me only with lip-service,*
> *while their hearts are far from me.*
> *Their reverence of me is worthless,*
> *The lessons they teach are nothing but human*
> *commandments."*

Matthew 15:1–9

Jesus once said to us, "Learn of me for I am meek and humble of heart." Meekness and humility are certainly fruits of the centering prayer. But we see here that meekness does not mean being a dishrag or a pushover. Meekness doesn't equal weakness. Jesus meets a challenging question with a challenging question, and some good, solid Scriptural argumentation. He does it out of love, not out of one-upmanship, hoping to help and enlighten his interlocutors, even though they may at this moment be coming after him with evil intent. Those who are meek with the meekness of the Beatitudes are courageous persons who do not hesitate to speak out when love demands it. They are not cowards in the face of human respect.

Another thing that is obvious here is Jesus' familiarity with the Scriptures. He undoubtedly heard them from his earliest years and began to learn them from memory before he could read. Then the Scriptures were his reader. As he learned to read, he read them. He recited portions of them each day. He listened to them in the synagogue weekly, in the temple at the great feasts. He sang them with others in these holy places and also along the roads and in the fields. They were woven deep into the fabric of his life, forming his human mind ever more in harmony with the divine.

From the hearing of the Scriptures comes faith and guidance as to how we are to respond to God and to each other. That is why in this book we have been listening to them to see what they might say about that response to God that we call centering prayer and about a centered life, the life that comes forth in us as a fruit of the regular practice of centering prayer. Regular *lectio*, meeting God in the Scriptures and listening to him, is a very important

part of a centered Christian life. When we practice centering prayer, we do not want to leave off the regular practice
of Scriptural prayer. Indeed, centering will create in us an
ever-greater desire to know God more and more and thus
send us eagerly to the Scriptures. Our meeting with him in
the Scriptures in its turn will increase our desire for that
intimate experiential contact we seek in centering prayer.

While it is then a certitude that we do not ever want to
leave Scriptural communion and prayer behind, it is also a
fact that when we begin to practice centering prayer, we
do usually leave behind other forms of prayer: some of our
vocal prayer practices, perhaps charismatic prayer and the
meetings where we shared that, maybe the rosary and
even the divine office.

This may be postulated simply by the exigencies of
time. We have just so many hours in the day and so many
things that have to be a part of our lives. I once asked the
Lord for a thirty-six-hour day. He replied that I mess up
twenty-four hours enough; he wasn't going to give me any
more time to mess up. Twenty-four hours are not enough,
but they are enough responsibility for most of us.

It is also true that we may not any longer need some of
these other forms of prayer. Or we may no longer find
them helpful. We do not want to see one form of prayer as
being better than another. But we do grow, and different
forms of prayer may better suit us, may be the better vehi-
cles for expressing our relationship with the Lord at different times in our lives.

It is at this point that the Pharisees and scribes might
come after us. *Why do you break away from the tradition of
the elders?* Every good Catholic says the rosary every day. If
you were really into Lent, you would make the stations of

the cross at least on Fridays. Didn't the Second Vatican Council say the office is *the* prayer? And so on.

And the Pharisee or scribe who might get after us most might well be ourselves.

Jesus points out a couple of very important things here. One of them was underlined by a recent synod at Rome. Social justice is a constitutive part of the Christian life, of living the Gospels. Any kind of prayer or practice that leads us to fail in justice to others is not Christian; it is not of Christ and his Spirit. It is not pleasing to God. True worship of God in spirit and truth will always move us not only to seek to be completely just in our dealing with others, but will also bear the fruits of love, kindness, long-suffering, goodness, and gentleness—fruits we sometimes very much need in caring for aging parents who have increasing needs as their humanity slips away from them. Here is where our prayer and practice meet their acid test. If we neglect giving our parents or anyone else the care that is due them in order to pray or to follow the customs and dictates of a hypocritically pious society, we are as far off base as those poor Pharisees and scribes, with their distorted traditions. *And our supposed reverence of God is worthless.*

There is a time, then, when the true needs of others make demands on us that do cut into our prayer time and other religous practices. When this is true of our parents, we can be happy that we are being given the opportunity to make some return to them for all the sacrifices they made for us when our true needs made such demands on them. Such a situation should not be forever and all-demanding. Every son and daughter has the right to get on with his or her own life, to follow his own vocation in life.

More than one monk or nun has had to leave the cloister
for a time to care for a needy parent, but it is for a time. It
is not always easy to judge what are legitimate demands.
We can err on one side or the other. Outside counsel is
sometimes really needed to see things objectively. Our
Lord points to what is more fundamental and necessary if
we are going to have any hope of making the right judgment in these matters.

Our service of the Lord cannot be merely something of
the lips, nor even just of the mind. It must be of the heart.
This is indeed the heart of the matter. Where is our heart
set? If our heart is truly set upon the Lord, then we will
want to be most faithful to our way of prayer, to a deep,
heartfelt union with God. And we will know that we can
lay aside our practices, and should, when true justice to
others calls for this, when an ordered love calls for it.

Centering prayer is prayer of the heart, prayer in the
heart. It completely leaves off the lip service. True centering prayer always disposes us to give everyone their due,
even while we cherish the time to give God his due. We
know the time of centering is needed and nourishing, the
source of all else. Yet we know that the call to constant
prayer is lived out in many ways, that our prayer can, and
does, take many forms. Sometimes our centering has to be
sitting by a bed, listening to each breath, ready to respond
to the least indication of need. Sometimes our centering
has to accept the interruptions of a parent who is losing it
and doesn't always stay settled for the twenty minutes we
try to center together. There are some days when we just
don't have twenty minutes to stop and center. And when
we do finally reach the end of the endless day and try to
center, we are almost immediately asleep. But we owe it to

ourselves, as well as to Christ and to all the other members of Christ for whom we live, not to allow situations like this to long prevail. Or we will soon find that our hearts are far from him, because we have been caught up in trying to honor him with doing and have lost our being.

Jesus tells us that it is the heart that matters. While we will pray in many different ways in the course of the day—communal prayer, liturgical prayer, shared Scripture, personal *lectio,* perhaps a rosary or the stations, frequent ejaculations, cries for help, and words of thanks—we will want to make time for the prayer of the heart, prayer in the heart. No one can practice centering prayer with any degree of fidelity and remain with their hearts far from God. As we faithfully let go of everything that comes along, everything from within and from without, to simply be to the Lord, all the dross and attachments wash away. I know of no other form of prayer that is so effective and so directly effective for helping us to arrive at purity of heart, so that instead of our hearts being far from the Lord, they are able to be wholly one with his wanting all that he wants. Then our reverence will be very precious to the Lord. Then we will live according to his commandments and not according to the customs and dictates of a hypocritical society. Then we will live from the heart.

Chapter 29

We Are Mothers
and We Are Dogs

Jesus left that place and withdrew to the region of Tyre and Sidon. And suddenly out came a Canaanite woman from that district and started shouting, "Lord, Son of David, take pity on me. My daughter is tormented by a devil." But he said not a word in answer to her. And his disciples went and pleaded with him, saying, "Give her what she wants, because she keeps shouting after us." He said in reply, "I was sent only to the lost sheep of the House of Israel." But the woman had come up and was bowing low before him. "Lord," she said, "help me." He replied, "It is not fair to take the children's food and throw it to little dogs." She retorted, "Ah yes, Lord; but even little dogs eat the scraps that fall from their masters' table." Then Jesus answered her, "Woman, you have great faith. Let your desire be granted." And from that moment her daughter was well again.

Matthew 15:21–28

In centering prayer we all become mothers, mothering the Christ within us and within the whole Body of Christ. The child within us, the Christ, seeks love, peace, quiet, well-being. But thoughts, feelings, desires pull us in every direction. The child within is "tormented"—though not by the devil.

People have sometimes expressed a fear that in opening ourselves completely as we do in centering prayer, we might be opening ourselves to the devil. Actually, we need have no fear here. "The kingdom of God is within." It is exclusively his. Only God can penetrate, can be, is, in fact, at the depths, the core, the heart, the center of our being, where he is constantly bringing us forth in his creative love. The evil one cannot gain entrance to the depths. The great teachers through the centuries, such as Saint John of the Cross, have very clearly taught this. The devil, in those rare cases of possession, takes possession only of the body. He cannot take possession of the soul. The only way he can influence the soul is through the body, especially through the feelings and emotions, for it is in this realm that the body and soul most intimately interact. This is why in a charismatic type of prayer, where feelings and emotions are very much a part of the prayer experience, there is quite legitimately a good bit of concern about the possibility of the evil one interjecting himself, producing counterfeit experiences. There is need for discernment as to what is the origin of the "lights" and feelings that one is receiving. In centering prayer, where we ignore all feelings and emotions and thoughts and images, we leave no place for the devil to influence our prayer.

The best way to demolish someone and his influence on us is to completely ignore him. If we argue with him or fight him, we at least acknowledge his existence and even that he is worth fighting. In centering prayer this is the way we handle the devil if he comes around and tries to influence us in one way or another. We totally ignore him. We treat him as a nonentity. And that takes care of him and any influence he might have upon us or our prayer.

Actually I don't think the devil has to bother with most of us. We are our own devil in the way we let the world and the flesh get hold of us. We are "tormented" enough by these.

When we go to centering prayer, we quite naturally look for some peace and quiet. We want to be released from the many discentering pulls the things of the world and the flesh exert on us. We rather hope we will not have to use our prayer word all the time, that thoughts and feelings will ease off and leave us in peace. But quite often that is not the case, especially when we first begin. There has been a buildup of tension in our psyche and body over how many years? There is a lot to be cleaned out. It is by the free flow of thoughts and feelings that this clearing-out is ordinarily accomplished. So the Lord leaves us "tormented" by many thoughts and feelings. He seems to *say not a word in answer,* to totally ignore us.

The rational intellect, that "disciple" of the Lord who is eager to tell the Lord how things should be done, keeps butting in. It goes looking for any reassuring feeling or bit of light it can find. It wants inner peace. It wants the Lord to intervene and quiet everything down. It wants his healing power to be evident.

What is Jesus' reply? "I was sent only to the lost sheep of the House of Israel." Jesus is saying two things here. That contemplation belongs to the members of the

"House of Israel" (the Church) and to those members who know themselves to be "lost sheep."

To most of Jesus' immediate hearers, when he said that his gifts were only for the House of Israel, they would have heard this as a rather excluding statement. They would not yet have grasped how the messianic times were at hand when all nations were being called to be of the House of Israel. Jesus' response to the woman, "Woman, you have great faith. Let your desire be granted," was an implicit statement of this messianic reality and also a declaration of the way one becomes a part of the messianic House of Israel—through faith.

Unfortunately, through many centuries, within this messianic House of Israel, the Church, another kind of exclusivity has been ascribed to Jesus. In practice, if not always in theory, Jesus' call to intimate friendship, to life within the Trinity, a bonding of deepest love, has been held as being addressed to a chosen few and not a universal call to all the members of the Church. Happily, the Second Vatican Council has made it most clear that all are called to intimate holiness, to the joys of contemplative union with the Lord.

But the only way in which we can respond to this call is in truth. And truth requires of us a deep spirit of humility.

Jesus puts the Canaanite woman down. He seems cruel. At times, the way he responds to us or fails to respond to us seems cruel. But it is a necessary cruelty, one inspired by love. It is meant to bring us to that self-knowledge which is the necessary precondition to accepting and being truth. Before we can approach the Lord in truth, we must come to know not only our sin and our need but our total unworthiness. Only then can Jesus safely give us the peace, the joy, the love, the life that we seek. Otherwise there is constant danger that we will think that these fruits of the Spirit are our own fruits, or at least that we in some way deserved to receive them.

The many times that centering prayer seems to be utterly fruitless, a humiliating exercise of total frustration, it is Jesus saying to us, "It is not fair to take the children's food and throw it to little dogs." Instead of being like the Prodigal Son, who readily admitted that he was not worthy of being a son, we can recoil from this—and give up our practice of centering prayer. We can decide that the way the Lord is responding to us just isn't right or, at least, proves we are not called to contemplative prayer, to a deep intimate union with God.

After all, we are the children of God; we are not dogs. But what we need to hang on to is the truth that we are children only by the totally gratuitous gift of baptism. By ourselves we are farther from the sublime dignity of the child of God than the dog is from our human dignity.

True humility is the key that opens the way to contemplation. In truth, we have to admit that we are dogs in the miserable way in which we have responded to an all-good and loving Father. At the same time, by his great mercy and grace, we are children, raised to the sublime dignity of sharing the divine nature and life. "He that is mighty has done great things for us." Knowing this mercy and love even as we know our sin, we can then come to the Lord in our centering prayer with the persistent faith and humility of the Canaanite woman.

And then our *desire will be granted.* Our spirit will no longer be tormented. The peace which the Lord alone can give will come upon us. Sure, we will still have many thoughts and feelings careening through as we sit in our prayer. But they won't bother us in the least. The torment comes from expecting things to be otherwise, thinking they should be otherwise, have to be, in order for our prayer to be "good," in order for us to be truly loved by God. In humility we will let go of all that and just be immensely happy and grateful that we are receiving the grace to sit there with the Lord, or at least wanting the Lord, a wanting that may not be at all in the feelings but just in the fact that we are sitting there. We will know what a sign of God's very special love for us it is that he gives us the grace to sit there regularly, faithfully. We will hear, by his grace and mercy, that "you have great faith" and we will know that ultimately all our desire will be granted.

Chapter 30

❖

We Are No One
but Jesus the Beloved

Six days later, Jesus took with him Peter and James and his brother John and led them up a high mountain by themselves. There in their presence he was tranfigured: his face shone like the sun and his clothes became as dazzling as light. And suddenly Moses and Elijah appeared to them; they were talking with him. Then Peter spoke to Jesus. "Lord," he said, "it is wonderful for us to be here, if you want me to, I will make three shelters here, one for you, one for Moses and one for Elijah." He was still speaking when suddenly a bright cloud covered them with shadow, and suddenly from the cloud there came a voice which said, "This is my Son, the Beloved; he enjoys my favor. Listen to him." When they heard this, the disciples fell on their faces, overcome with fear. But Jesus came up and touched them, saying, "Stand up, do not be afraid." And when they raised their eyes they saw no one but Jesus.

Matthew 17:1–8

The Lord has his favorites. Sometimes, especially we egalitarian Americans, think that God should treat us all equally. He doesn't. He gives different talents, different graces, different blessings to each. Among the Twelve, Peter, James, and John were favorites. Among his disciples today, you are one of his favorites. He has called you to the intimacy of contemplative prayer and has given you the grace to respond. May that grace ever grow in you.

On the particular occasion Matthew tells us about here, Jesus invited the three chosen ones to a special sharing, a special grace of experience. And they responded.

It wasn't that easy for them. For one thing, they didn't know where he was actually leading them. And it was a tough climb.

Even today Tabor is a special place of prayer and encounter with the Lord. A real sanctuary. The mount, which stands out above all the surrounding plains, is so steep that the tourist buses cannot ascend. So it is only the true pilgrim who makes the arduous journey to the top.

Peter, James, and John, with faith and trust in the Lord, followed him. "And suddenly Moses and Elijah appeared to them." Moses was the great lawgiver, and Elijah, the great prophet. When the Jews speak of the Sacred Scriptures, they speak of them as "the Law and the Prophets." The meaning of this encounter here for us is that it is through the Scriptures we are prepared to see the Christ. We need our regular *lectio* if we want to come to a Taboric experience of the Lord in our centering prayer.

The three disciples did respond to the Lord. They followed him in faith. Their commitment was very real. They persevered through the tough climb. Then "in their presence he was transfigured." If we persevere in our daily practice of centering prayer, we, too, will come to see the Lord in some wondrous new way, through the operation of the Holy Spirit in the gifts of knowledge, understanding, and wisdom.

The evangelists struggle to describe this experience of Christ: "his face shone like the sun and his clothes became dazzling as light"; "his clothes became brilliantly white, whiter than any earthly bleacher could make them" (Mark); "the aspect of his face was changed and his clothing became sparkling white" (Luke). It is certainly one of light, a light not of this world, a light too bright for the human eye. The experiences of God that we have in centering prayer are quite literally beyond us. We see their effect in our lives. They shed oblique light on everything else that is of faith, everything in the creation. But the experience itself is beyond what our human mind or memory can contain or retain. All we know is that something deep within us says, "Lord, it is wonderful for us to be here."

I really like Peter. He is such an impulsive, hearty human being. Rushing in where angels fear to tread, he usually ends up putting his foot in his own mouth. If God can make a great saint out of the likes of him, then there's hope for the rest of us.

So, like us, Peter can't just rest in the wonder of the Lord, rest in the center. He has to be saying something, doing something. The false self is still very much there. "I will make three shelters [the type of booth the Jews make during the fall festival when they share again mystically the journey into the Promised Land] here, one for you, one for Moses and one for Elijah." Saint Luke in his account adds quite cryptically, "He didn't know what he was talking about." That is certainly true of us. As Saint Paul assures us, "We do not know how to pray as we ought." Yet our mind just keeps on trying to run the show. Here is where the method of centering prayer so helps us. It gives us a means, that simple little word of love, to leave the babbling behind and rest in the wondrous reality.

"A bright cloud covered them with shadow." This sounds almost like a contradiction. A "bright" cloud should enlighten rather than leave us in greater darkness. But this is somewhat our experience in centering prayer, at least initially. One of the earliest and best known treatises on this kind of prayer in the English language is *The Cloud of Unknowing*. The Divine Light, the illumination that we experience, makes us realize that our poor rational intellect knows little or nothing about things divine. We get to know our darkness.

When we are willing to accept this and rest in it, waiting and listening, then we, too, hear the Father speaking in the silence—God speaks by silence—"This is my Child, the Beloved; he enjoys my favor."

We hear the Father say this to us of his Son, our Lord Jesus. Jesus has told us that "no one knows the Son but the Father and the one to whom he reveals him." The Father reveals his beloved Son to us. We come to know Jesus in the fullness of his being and not just in the flesh. We come to know something of the inner life of the Trinity. We come to learn how to truly listen to the Son, how to allow him to enter our life in all his fullness, no longer limited by the limitations of our own poor created and very limited listening.

Sometimes people have had difficulty with the idea of centering prayer because they feared it was leaving Jesus behind. They quote Saint Teresa of Jesus to the effect that she always began her prayer by approaching Jesus in his agonizing humanity. That was her way, and it really worked for her. But each should be free to follow the way the Lord leads him or her. If we are truly being to the Lord, we will never leave Jesus behind. He enjoys the Father's favor. The Father will always point us toward his Beloved: "Listen to him" with your whole being. Be totally open to him. Let him truly live in and through you. Be one with him.

And this is another message we receive from the Father. For he says to us, speaking of us, "This is my Child, my Beloved; the one who enjoys my favor." In this prayer we come to know, as we see ourselves reflected back in the eyes of the Lover-God, that we are his beloved child, that his favor does rest on us.

In the midst of all this "the disciples fell on their faces, overcome with fear." It is not uncommon that we experience some fear in centering prayer. We are dying to the false self, and it is frightening to die, especially if we do not yet know the true self. Death is death. We are also being brought more deeply and intimately into the presence of the divine. This is awesome and fearful. The whole territory is strange. There are thoughts and feeling flying in all directions. I like the classic icon of the Transfiguration. It shows Jesus surrounded by all the colors of the rainbow, a radiant splendor. Below him on the rocky mountaintop are the three disciples, sprawled out in different directions, their sandals flying. It is a good depiction of our experience in the prayer.

And when it was over, "they saw no one but Jesus." Through centering prayer not only do we come to know

Jesus in the fullness of his divinity but we also come to know Jesus in the fullness of his humanity, in his oneness with every other human person. Through the activity of the Holy Spirit in her gifts, we begin to see Jesus in everyone and everyone in Jesus. It would be hard to overstate the love and joy that this brings into our lives. And how it effects all our human relations, all our ministerial outreach, all our presence to others.

Centering prayer is meant to lead all the way to the summit of the Taboric experience. And it will infallibly lead there if one is faithful in following Jesus, even though we don't know where he is leading us, until he does deign to be transfigured in our presence. If we remain faithfully in our prayer, whether it be experienced as a solitary mountaintop, an illuminating experience of Christ and the Scriptures, or a cloud of unknowing that overshadows us, we will come to hear the Father say to us of us, "This is my child, my beloved; the one who enjoys my favor."

Appendix

Centering Prayer

Centering prayer is a very simple way of prayer and can be used by anyone who wants to be with God, to experience his love and presence. It is a prayer of longing that leads into a prayer of presence.

First of all, we settle down quietly. Most of us pray best sitting down, but take any posture that works well for you. It is best if the back is fairly straight and well supported. If we gently close our eyes, we immediately begin to quiet down, for we use a lot of our psychic energy in seeing.

Once we are settled, we turn our attention to the Lord present within us. We know he is there by faith; that is, we know he is there because he said so. In love we turn ourselves over to him. For these minutes we are all his. He can do with us whatever he wants. This prayer is a pure gift, a gift of self in love.

In order to be able to abide quietly and attentively with our Beloved, we use a love word, a prayer word—a simple word that expresses our being to the Lord in love. It might well be our favorite name for him: Lord, Jesus, Father,

Love—whatever is meaningful for us. We just let that word be there, to keep us attentive to him. It is not an effortful ejaculation or a constantly repeated mantra, but rather a sigh of love, a murmur of love, a "being to."

Whenever, during the time of our prayer, we become aware of anything else, we simply use our love word to return to the Lord. Some days we will have to use the word a great deal: there may be a lot of commotion around us or in us. No matter. Each time we use it, each time we return to him, it is a perfect gift of self to him in love. Other days we may not need to use our word much at all. Fine! It really makes no difference. Simply, these minutes are all his to do with as he likes. We don't seek anything for ourselves. It is pure gift. It is not during the prayer that we will be aware of things. All our attention is on him. It is outside the time of prayer that we will begin to see the difference, as the fruits of the Spirit—love, peace, joy, kindness—begin to flourish in our lives.

At the end of our twenty minutes, we do not want to jump right back into activity. We have gone very deep, even if we don't seem to sense it. So we want to end our prayer very gently. I suggest praying interiorly, very slowly, using the Our Father. Let each phrase come forth with all its meaning. In this the Lord will teach us much. And the deep peace of our contemplative prayer will flow into our active lives.

It is a prayer of experience, so we can only know it by experience. We always urge people learning this prayer to make a commitment to themselves to practice the prayer faithfully, twice a day, for at least thirty days.

A SUMMARY

This simple traditional method of being to the Lord may be summed up thus:

> Sit relaxed and quiet.

1. Be in faith and love to God who dwells in the center of your being.

2. Take up a love word and let it be gently present, supporting your being to God in faith-filled love.

3. Whenever you become aware of anything, simply, gently return to the Lord with the use of your prayer word.

> Let the Our Father pray itself within you.

Select Bibliography

BOOKS

Abhisktananda (Fr. Henri Le Saux, OSB), *Prayer* (Philadelphia: Westminster Press, 1973).

Anonymous, *The Cloud of Unknowing and the Book of Privy Counseling*, ed. William Johnston (Garden City, N.Y.: Doubleday, 1973).

Benson, Herbert, *Relaxation Response* (New York: William Morrow, 1975).

——, *Beyond the Relaxation Response* (New York: Time Books, 1984).

Bloom, Anthony, *Living Prayer* (Springfield, Ill.: Templegate Publishers, 1966).

——, *Beginning to Pray* (Mahwah, N.J.: Paulist Press, 1971).

Chariton of Valamo, *The Art of Prayer* (London: Faber and Faber, 1966).

Dalrymple, John, *Simple Prayer* (Wilmington, Del.: Michael Glazier, 1984).

Evagrius Ponticus, *Praktikos: Chapters on Prayer* (Kalamazoo, Mich.: Cistercian Publications, 1970).

Griffiths, Bede, *Return to the Center* (Springfield, Ill.: Templegate Publishers, 1976).

Hausherr, Irenee, *The Name of Jesus* (Kalamazoo, Mich.: Cistercian Publications, 1978).

Higgins, John J., *Thomas Merton on Prayer* (Garden City, N.Y.: Doubleday, 1972).

Hodgson, Phyllis, ed. *Deonise Hid Divinite and Other Treatises on Contemplative Prayer Related to the Cloud of Unknowing* (London: Oxford University Press, 1958).

John of the Cross, *The Collected Works* (Washington, D.C.: ICS Publications, 1973).

Johnston, William, *The Stillpoint* (New York: Fordham University Press, 1970).

————, *Silent Music* (New York: Harper & Row, 1974).

————, *The Mysticism of the Cloud of Unknowing* (St. Meinrad, Ind.: Abbey Press, 1975).

————, *The Inner Eye of Love* (San Francisco: Harper & Row, 1978).

Kadloubowsky, E., and G. E. H. Palmer, ed. *Early Fathers from the Philokalia* (London: Faber and Faber, 1954).

Keating, Thomas, *At the Heart of the World* (New York: Crossroad Publishing, 1982).

————, *Open Mind, Open Heart* (Warwick, N.Y.: Amity House, 1985).

Keating, Thomas, et al., *Finding Grace at the Center* (Still River, Mass.: St. Bede's Publications, 1978).

Lawrence, Brother, *Practice of the Presence of God* (Springfield, Ill.: Templegate Publishers, 1974).

Louf, Andre, *Teach Us to Pray* (Mahwah, N.J.: Paulist Press, 1978).

Main, John, *Moment of Christ: The Path of Meditation* (London: Darton, Longmans and Todd, 1984).

Maloney, George, *Inward Stillness* (Denville, N.J.: Dimension Books, 1976).

Merton, Thomas, *New Seeds of Contemplation* (New York: New Directions, 1961).

————, *The New Man* (New York: Farrar, Straus and Giroux, 1961).

————, *Contemplative Prayer* (Garden City, N.Y.: Doubleday, 1971).

————, *Contemplation in a World of Action* (Garden City, N.Y.: Doubleday, 1973).

Naranjo, C., and R. E. Ornstein, *On the Psychology of Meditation* (New York: Viking, 1971).

Nemeck, Francis Kelly, and Marie Theresa Coombs, *Contemplation* (Wilmington, Del.: Michael Glazier, 1982).

Pennington, M. Basil, *Daily We Touch Him* (Garden City, N.Y.: Doubleday, 1977).

————, *Centering Prayer* (Garden City, N.Y.: Doubleday, 1980).

————, *Challenges in Prayer* (Wilmington, Del.: Michael Glazier, 1982).

————, *A Place Apart* (Garden City, N.Y.: Doubleday, 1983).

————, *Centered Living* (Garden City, N.Y.: Doubleday, 1986).

Richards, M. C., *Centering in Poetry, Poetry and the Person* (Middletown, Conn.: Wesleyan University Press, 1964).

Teresa of Ávila, *Interior Castle* (Garden City, N.Y.: Doubleday, 1961).

————, *The Way of Perfection* (Garden City, N.Y.: Doubleday, 1964).

William of Saint Thierry, *On Contemplating God, Prayer, Meditations* (Kalamazoo, Mich.: Cistercian Publications, 1977).

ARTICLES

Clark, Thomas, "Finding Grace at the Center," in *The Way,* vol. 17 (1977), pp. 12–22.

Gilles, Anthony E., "Three Modes of Meditation," in *America,* vol. 139 (1978), pp. 52–54.

Keating, Thomas, "Contemplative Prayer in the Christian Tradition," in *America,* vol. 138 (1978), pp. 278–281.

————, "Cultivating the Centering Prayer," in *Review for Religious,* vol. 37 (1978), pp. 10–15.

————, "Meditative Prayer," in *Today's Catholic Teacher,* vol. 12, no. 5 (Feb. 1979), pp. 32–33.

Llewelyn, Robert, "The Positive Role of Distractions in Prayer," in *Fairacres Chronicle,* vol. 8, no. 2 (Summer, 1975), pp. 22–29.

————, "The Treatment of Distractions in Zen and *The Cloud of Unknowing,*" in *Fairacres Chronicle,* vol. 16, no. 3 (Winter, 1983), pp. 7–20.

Main, John, "Prayer in the Tradition of John Cassian," in *Cistercian Studies,* vol. 12 (1977), pp. 184–190, 272–281; and vol. 13 (1978), pp. 75–83.

Merton, Thomas, "The Inner Experience," in *Cistercian Studies,* vol. 18 (1983), pp. 3–15, 121–134, 201–216, 289–300; and vol. 19 (1984), pp. 62–78, 139–150, 267–282, 336–345.

Nouwen, Henri, "Unceasing Prayer," in *America,* vol. 139 (1978), pp. 46–51.

Pennington, M. Basil, "Centering Prayer—Prayer of Quiet," in *Review for Religious,* vol. 35 (1976), pp. 651–662.

————, "TM and Christian Prayer," in *Pastoral Life,* vol. 25 (1976), pp. 9–16.

————, "Listening to the Fathers," in *Spiritual Life,* vol. 24 (1978), pp. 12–17.

————, "Centering Prayer: The Christian Privilege," in *Emmanuel,* vol. 85 (1979), pp. 61–68.

INTERVIEWS

Bernier, Paul, "Conversation with Basil Pennington," in *Emmanuel,* vol. 85 (1979), pp. 69–86.

Heffern, Rich, "Centering Prayer—A Way to Pray, A Way to Live: An Interview with Basil Pennington," in *Praying,* no. 24 (1988), pp. 22–28.

O'Connor, Liz, "Father Pennington and the Centering Prayer," in *Catholic Digest,* vol. 44, no. 7 (May 1980), pp. 95–98.

AUDIO CASSETTES

Johnston, William, "Contemplative Prayer" (Kansas City, Mo.: National Catholic Reporter, 1983).

Keating, Thomas, "Contemplative Prayer in the Christian Tradition: Historical Insights" (Spencer, Mass.: Saint Joseph's Abbey, 1978).

Main, John, "Christian Meditation: Our Oldest and Newest Form of Prayer" (Kansas City, Mo.: National Catholic Reporter, 1981).

Meninger, William, "Contemplative Prayer" (Liguori, Mo.: Liguori Press, 1975).

Pennington, M. Basil, "A Centered Life: A Practical Course on Centering Prayer" (Kansas City, Mo.: National Catholic Reporter, 1981).

————, "The Contemplative Attitude" (Kansas City, Mo.: National Catholic Reporter, 1981).

————, "Cottage Talks" (Kansas City, Mo.: National Catholic Reporter, 1984).

————, "Centering Prayer Retreat" (Fort Lauderdale, Fla.: Harfoot Tape Ministry, 1985).

VIDEO CASSETTES

Keating, Thomas, "The Spiritual Journey," 22 conferences (Colorado Springs, Colo.: Contemporary Communications).

Pennington, M. Basil, "Contemplation for Everyone," 3 conferences (Pompano Beach, Fla.: Food for the Poor).

————, "Faith: Journey to the Center," 6 conferences (Kansas City, Mo.: Credence Cassettes).

————, "How To Center Your Life," 4 conferences (Allen, Tex.: Argus Communications).

————, "A Matter of Love," 4 conferences (Kansas City, Mo.: Credence Cassettes).

————, "Opening the Contemplative Dimension" (Kansas City, Mo.: Credence Cassettes).

About the Author

M. Basil Pennington, O.C.S.O., is a Cistercian (Trappist) monk and Abbot of Assumption Abbey in Ava, Missouri. He travels extensively to conduct workshops on Centering Prayer and is the author of several books, including *Centering Prayer* and *Daily We Touch Him*.